REFLECTIONS ON
Creating Your Luminous Life

Books by Cheryl Lafferty Eckl

Memoirs of Transformation
A Beautiful Death: Keeping the Promise of Love
A Beautiful Grief: Reflections on Letting Go
Reflections on Ineffable Love: from loss through grief to joy

Self-Transcendence with Your Wise Inner Counselor
The LIGHT Process: Living on the Razor's Edge of Change
Reflections on Being Your True Self in Any Situation
Reflections on Doing Your Great Work in Any Occupation
Reflections on Creating Your Luminous Life:
Self-Transcendence from the Inside Out

Mystical Poetry for Inspiration & Beauty
Poetics of Soul & Fire
Bridge to the Otherworld
Idylls from the Garden of Spiritual Delights & Healing
Sparks of Celtic Mystery: soul poems from Éire
A Beautiful Joy: Reunion with the Beloved
Through Transfiguring Love

Spiritual Romance Novels for the Love of Twin Flames
The Weaving:
A Novel of Twin Flames Through Time

Twin Flames of Éire Trilogy
The Ancients and The Call
The Water and The Flame
The Mystics and The Mystery

The Mystical Thread:
a legacy of love - past, present & future

A Wise Inner Counselor Book

REFLECTIONS ON
Creating Your Luminous Life

SELF-TRANSCENDENCE
FROM THE INSIDE OUT

Cheryl Lafferty Eckl

FLYING CRANE PRESS

REFLECTIONS ON CREATING YOUR LUMINOUS LIFE:
SELF-TRANSCENDENCE FROM THE INSIDE OUT
Copyright © 2024, 2026 by Cheryl J. Eckl, LLC
A Wise Inner Counselor™ Book
Wise Inner Counselor™

Published by Flying Crane Press
Livingston, Montana 59047
Cheryl@CherylEckl.com | www.CherylEckl.com

Library of Congress Control Number: 2021922036
ISBN: 978-1-7367123-5-1 (paperback)
ISBN: 978-1-7367123-6-8 (ebook)
ISBN: 978-1-7367123-7-5 (audiobook)

Any images not from the author's personal collection are licensed royalty-free from 123rf.com, Alamy, Bigstock, GettyImages.com, istock.com, Shutterstock, are used by permission of the artist or photographer, or are in the public domain.

All rights reserved. No part of this publication may be reproduced, distributed, or transmitted in any form or by any means whatsoever, including photocopying, recording, or other electronic or mechanical methods, or by any AI training technologies, without the prior written permission of the author or publisher, except in the case of brief quotations embodied in critical reviews and certain other noncommercial uses permitted by copyright law.

Written and narrated by the author. Not by AI.

The information and insights in this book are solely the opinion of the author and should not be considered as a form of therapy, advice, direction, diagnosis and/or treatment of any kind. This information is not a substitute for medical, psychological or other professional advice, counseling, or care. All matters pertaining to your individual health should be supervised by an appropriate healthcare practitioner. Neither the author nor the publisher assumes any responsibility or liability whatsoever on behalf of any purchaser or reader.

*For you who know
there is more*

*On the journey
of transcendence
we pour into our endeavors
wisdom of the inner guide—
the luminous flame
of our highest aspirations.*

Contents

Part One ~ A Vision of Transcendence
Sparking the Fire of Inner Knowing

1	The Hero of Your Story	3
2	An Ineffable Ocean of Beingness	5
3	Seeking the Transcendent Self	9
4	A Transcending Universe	13
5	Journeying Up & In	17
6	The Perpetual Thread of Contact	21
7	Our Heritage of Transcendence	25
8	Reflecting on Your Luminous Life - 1	31

Part Two ~ The Need for Transcendence
Inside Maslow's Psychology of Being

9	Why Study Maslow?	37
10	Maslow the Transcender	40
11	Essentials of Motivation	47
12	At the Heart of Maslow	55
13	The Way of Love Knowledge	61
14	Living in Being-Cognition	66
15	Entering Mystical Being	73
16	Reflecting on Your Luminous Life - 2	79

Part Three ~ Lighting a Candle in the Dark
Outwitting the Shadow Self

17	Digging Deep, Reaching High	83
18	No Sympathy for the Shadow	88
19	The Danger of Collectives	94
20	Metapathologies - Cause or Effect?	98
21	One of the Biggest Obstacles	103
22	The Miracle of Invoking Light	107
23	Reflecting on Your Luminous Life - 3	113

Part Four ~ Creativeness Is Transcending
Bringing Your Light to Life

24	Musing on the Mystery	119
25	Opening to Creativeness	125
26	Seeking the "Growing Tip"	129
27	Actualizing Our Creativeness	134
28	Spirals of Creativeness	138
29	Creativeness in Loss	145
30	Our Soul's Greatest Creation	149
31	Reflecting on Your Luminous Life - 4	155

Part Five ~ Ascending the Spiral of Being
Strengthening the Thread of Contact

32	To Live in Wonder	159
33	A Passion for the Summit	163
34	Mirror of the Over-Soul	167
35	The Right to Be Divine	171

36	Service as a Calling	175
37	Transcending in the Unitive	179
38	Transcending with Your Soul's Twin	187
39	A Rhapsody of Transcendence	192
40	Reflecting on Your Luminous Life - 5	194

Part Six ~ Resources for Your Journey
More ~ For New Beginnings

41	Appendix A: Enhancing Your Transcendence	199
42	Appendix B: Being Transcendent & Resilient	207

Notes	216
Acknowledgements	221
About the Author	223

PART ONE

A Vision of Transcendence

Sparking the Fire of Inner Knowing

*Trust the light of Spirit
that stirs
in your deepest heart
as you awaken
to your transcendent Self.*

Chapter One

The Hero of Your Story

Every good story needs a hero or heroine. An admirable character around whom the action revolves. The navigator who, with laser-like focus, masters life's most treacherous waters to bring the voyagers safely home. The scout who blazes a trail through a wilderness of chaos and confusion. The intrepid Sherpa who guides courageous climbers to and from the summit.

There are many stories contained in these pages. The hero whose light beats in the heart of each central character is the True Self—the luminous presence I call the Wise Inner Counselor.[1]

The Self Upon Whom We Rely

Timeless as the Eternal Now, this inner wise one is your soul's best friend, the source of your creativeness, the spiritual dynamo that empowers you to transcend your limited self.

You may know this presence as the still small voice of conscience or intuition. You may have experienced its immeasurable compassion as inspiration for better choices than you otherwise might have made. Or perhaps you have been warned not to take a step that could have been disastrous.

Beyond the illusions of personality, you may recognize the inner guide as an intimate companion whose knowledge of you far exceeds your human mind's ability to comprehend.

Like an eternal pilot light, this interior spark is a fragment of spirit substance that lives within you. It is a drop of Infinity's ocean—different in size, yet equal in quality. It has access to your soul, to your Highest Self, and to the blueprint of your unique identity.

In the midst of swirling thoughts or emotions, your divine pilot can pull you to safety in the hurricane's calm eye. On the high seas of life, this unfailing lover of your soul is the captain of your ship, your lifeline to reality.

Our Story Unites Us

Speaking as the voice of Love, your Wise Inner Counselor is the unifying spirit that can harmonize your soul's fondest dreams with the necessities of daily existence while lifting you into the virtue, honor, and nobility that are the essences from which your luminous life is created.

This sunlit presence holds the vision of your brightest future and urges you to follow your heart into the oneness that is home to your True Self.

For, though forces of enmity and suspicion may attempt to divide us, our hearts are united in a shared heroic story—the transcendent journey we are invited to embark upon together, now with a mystic's inside-out perspective.

Inviting Your Reflections

If we were gathered at one of my retreats or workshops, we would pause occasionally to share any thoughts or feelings that might arise as we make our way along the path of self-transcendence.

Perhaps one day we will be together for a live event. Until then, I invite you to enjoy the opportunities for self-reflection that I have included at the end of each main section of the book. And if you do want to share your thoughts, please feel free to contact me through my website at www.cheryleckl.com.

Chapter Two

An Ineffable Ocean of Being

How do you write about a quality of your being that is so much a part of you that you really cannot describe it? That has been my constant challenge in compiling this book.

I am a bit like the proverbial fish who asks, "What's water?" Transcendence is the ineffable ocean of being in which I swim. So, how do I step onto dry land long enough to watch and listen for what I might learn from the rhythmic sights and sounds of waves cresting and rolling to shore?

Ever so briefly, I stand with my feet on wet sand, gazing at far vistas of sea and sky. And then I feel it. My soul's longing for the ineffable ocean. She loves its ephemeral water.

And so, I give myself up to the transcendent waves of being and smile as my soul shares her ecstatic delight in the experience.

Imagining Transcendence

When I think of transcendence, an image comes to mind of a photo taken when I was around three years old. I remember imagining I could fly. I certainly contained enough enthusiasm to sprout wings. Nowadays, when I contemplate transcendence, I think of a similar joy, though one that has matured through years of earnest spiritual seeking and grateful finding.

I experience transcendence as a voyage into the heart where my Wise Inner Counselor may appear more vibrantly with each new day as I rise with the sun, absorb its radiance into my

being, and give voice to its golden beams of illumination in all my words and deeds.

I experience transcendence as a dynamic state that moves me along on a journey that contains everything I need to liberate my soul from negative patterns of past and present, or from a stifling future that is inevitable without spiritual progress.

Being transcendent creates in me an expanded perception of the truth of my being, an ability to love more selflessly, and a sense of empowerment that increases as I partner with a cosmic will that wants only the best for me.

When I tap into the innate enthusiasm that sent my three-year-old self winging her way into an unknown future, I feel my heart burn as a beacon that shines a light on the spiritual path I am called to walk.

Entering Deeply into Transcendence

Out of my soul's yearning, my Wise Inner Counselor lets me know that transcendence is not understood in separation. Only by entering in more deeply than my previous sojourns into the mystery of Self will the vastnesses of this transfiguring power reveal themselves.

For transcendence is exultation, joy, deep inner knowing of truths that are more felt than spoken. Beyond human, here is transfiguration, divine inspiration. Slipping through the veil of time into the spaciousness of ethereal realms.

Transcendence goes beyond whatever form or concept can be named. To transcend is to move through obstacles of seeming limitation to etheric dimensions where thoughts and emotions merge into universal oneness.

Transcendence offers a deepening into divine beauty that elevates all it touches and restores my soul to her natural state of innocent transparency.

And perhaps most importantly and tangibly, to transcend is to pursue a path of practical spirituality that makes me more effective in my daily life.

Creating My Luminous Life

I have come to know transcendence as the nature of my Wise Inner Counselor. The essence of one is the essence of the other.

As I overcome the fearful self who forgot the exuberant child she once was, I become more authentic. As I grow into deeper communion with the loving inner adult who cherishes that child, I become more transcendent.

And day by day my being fills up with the realization of the unity my soul has longed for. Where an uncertain traveler once wandered, a well-grounded mystic now lives a luminous life.

Chapter Three

Seeking the Transcendent Self

Who am I? How many of us have asked that question? How many of us continue inquiring into the heart of our being? This is a sure sign of transcendence in action. When we know in our bones that there is more to us than appearance or accomplishment, we never stop asking.

As a freshman in college, I remember being shocked by the question of identity. In fact, I got the worst grades of my life that year because I spent more hours in late-night conversations with my dormmates than I did in studying.

Like many, I had sailed off to college thinking I knew who I was. But that persona was largely a product of other people's concepts of me, which I had learned to accommodate. Now when I asked, "Who am I?" I realized I didn't have a clue. Forging a genuine identity was topmost in my mind.

Missing the Theme of My Early Life

Perhaps only time and maturity offer enough distance from our younger selves to see what lies within.

What I couldn't perceive as a college freshman was the theme of my first eighteen years of life. I had always been in hot pursuit of what was next and what was "more." And the next "more" was usually spiritual, even when I thought it wasn't.

My childhood had been peppered with flashes of insight into other planes of being. Sensory experiences convinced me that ethereal realms were real and that it was possible to have friends in Spirit. My Grandma Cody had such friends and I could feel them around her when we were together.

By the age of nine, I knew I wanted to live with the same kind of otherworldly communion. I realize now that I recognized Grandma Cody's connection with spiritual realms because I was already transcending my way through this world. For some years a wise inner identity had been making itself known to me in unexpected inspirations and occasional visions.[2]

Finding "More"

Despite my teens and twenties being surfeited in a social and academic climate that seemed intent on negating my connection with the deep mysteries of soul and spirit, the interior voice did continue to call me—sometimes faintly and at other times with undeniable intensity.

However, I was still in the dark about my identity. The fact is that I did not gain an understanding of my True Self until I studied transpersonal psychology, which had been developed by Dr. Abraham H. Maslow[3] as the final triumph of his life that ended suddenly in 1970.

Throughout his career, he focused on evolving a positive, holistic approach to human psychology. What he brilliantly accomplished in his deep dive into the secrets of selfhood was the articulation in psychological terms of experiences and states of awareness that previously had been the purview of religion, philosophy, and sacred texts from ages past.

Dr. Maslow spent many years observing individuals he identified as psychologically healthy and fully human—meaning those who more completely actualized their potential than did most others.

He determined that some people possess a powerful motivation to live in what he called "Being-cognition"—a state of consciousness that is psychologically grounded, inwardly aware, and highly attuned to the present moment. Initially, these were his "self-actualizers."

When I studied Maslow's work in graduate school, I learned that his theory of human motivation had expanded to include the unique group that was prompted to access dimensions of awareness that were beyond average human experience. He called them "self-transcenders" and their psychology "transpersonal."

I deeply resonated with Maslow's perspective. At last, here was the "more" I had been seeking.

Chapter Four

A Transcending Universe

I do not remember when I first learned that the universe is expanding. I know the revelation came to me years ago and that I was not really surprised. What did amaze me was the notion that the Divine is also perpetually exceeding its former state.

The concept made sense. If our human creations are a reflection of our consciousness, then a dynamic universe could come only from a creator who is transcendent.

If we are created in that cosmic image, the desire and the ability to continually transform our former self must be a key facet of our true identity. We share with every new star in our galaxy the essence of limitless being.

Exceeding the Past

Transcendence is physical, not merely metaphysical. In our desire to exceed the past, we strive for engagement with the fullness of life, not escape from the mundane.

We begin to realize that our automatic, conditioned responses to life have compounded into a fearful, egoic imposter of our True Self that has stifled us for far too long.

We start consciously building upon what is wisest, noblest, and truest about us so that each phase of our journey may include and then surmount our previous accomplishments.

Picking Up the Pace

Throughout my life I have found myself in situations that demanded my surpassing what I thought I could accomplish. I would be challenged to bring to bear all of my skills and presence of mind and heart. When I managed to dig deep and reach high, I often produced astonishing results.

In the aftermath of what seemed miraculous, I would feel an even stronger urge to pick up the pace of my personal growth and increase my capabilities in order to be better prepared for the next challenge, which I knew would arrive. The unexpected is always just around the corner.

"Be Ready" is now my motto. As accelerating my attunement with spiritual promptings has become my practice, I have discovered that one of the best ways for me to be prepared for unexpected events is to make time and space for contemplation.

Reflection as an Open Door

I am a "make-it-happen" kind of person with a very active mind. Sitting meditation does not come easily to me, although ever since I can remember, I have been listening for inspiration.

Over the years these periods of reflection have created an open door, bringing me profound insights I can rely on. I have not always made good decisions. Yet, when I connect with an interior serenity, my choices are much wiser.

A Poetical Theme

I find the verses of William Wordsworth relevant here. In his classic poem *Lines Composed a Few Miles above Tintern Abbey*, he describes a sublime experience of silence.

He glides seamlessly from his recollections of physical landscape to the interior beauty of:

> sensations sweet,
> Felt in the blood, and felt along the heart,
> And passing even into my purer mind
> With tranquil restoration

Later in the poem he writes the lines that confirm my childhood practice of listening and that have continued to inspire me for many years:

> While with an eye made quiet by the power
> Of harmony and the deep power of joy,
> We see into the life of things.[4]

Here is a poetical theme that has appeared in the mind and heart of saints, sages, seekers, and seers past and present. For it is the True Self who sees into the life of things.

"Look deeper," I can hear inner guidance encouraging us. "Let your gaze flow from the temporal to the eternal and then you may see into the life of your own reality."

The Opportunity of a Lifetime

You are made of starlight and that radiance lives within you. You have direct, intuitive access to that presence who speaks to you as Love. Listen carefully and you may hear the voice of your Wise Inner Counselor whispering a secret known to illumined people of all ages:

> The purpose of self-transcendence is to become the ever-expanding light that is your essence—pure and simple—and the opportunity of a lifetime.

Chapter Five

Journeying Up & In

Inner guidance urges us to flow like water. To rise with the morning tides. To ride the stream of beingness that is uniquely ours to navigate. To trust that the Spirit which animates our life understands how this journey takes us both up and in.

Up to new heights of consciousness, where who we have been yields to who we really are. And purposefully in to that awareness. Our journey's pilot knows the way. Our task is to watch and listen and continue onward, moment by moment, step by determined step.

An Interviewer Wants to Know

In a recent podcast interview, I was explaining that the common theme that runs through my books is the presence of my Wise Inner Counselor and my commitment to following its lead.

The interviewer remarked that she really could have used such a counselor. She couldn't recall ever having heard that voice.

She was obviously someone who was following an intuitive prompting to create the podcast that was becoming her full-time job. The fact that she was not consciously aware of her own inner guide caught my attention.

Guarding the Unseen

I shared with her that most of us get talked out of contact with our inherent wisdom early in life. Many children see angels or elemental beings such as fairies and gnomes. If they are wise enough to keep the existence of their invisible friends to themselves, they may develop a keen awareness of being nurtured by spiritual light and love.

However, if in their enthusiasm they talk about their experiences to adults or even to older children who have lost their own vision, the little seers may be dismissed, chastised, or worse.

I remember telling my mother about my guardian angel. She did not disparage my story, but she also did not encourage what she may have considered a fantasy. As I grew into adolescence, my sense of that presence waned. Only years later did I realize its importance.

Innocence Is Inner Sense

The innocence of children is meant to keep them connected with the tangible presence of their Wise Inner Counselor—to nurture their confidence in that connection and to encourage them to retain it.

All too often that inborn link to their inner guide is thwarted by noise, menacing cartoon characters, or sexually explicit images that are promoted by parents, teachers, or others who themselves may have been discouraged from the heart communion that can foster a balanced psyche.

Do we even say, "Out of the mouths of babes" these days? Or has society so successfully shut the door on the unspoiled innocence of childhood that little ones no longer have access to the wisdom that is supposed to flow to them unfettered?

Young children do not have the cerebral development to comprehend complex issues of identity. What they do have is an inner teacher who can guide them into becoming psychologically healthy individuals. That is, if they are encouraged to follow their souls' longing for wholeness, rather than the pied pipers of modern culture whose intentions are not benign.

What Children Know

When allowed to do so, very small children may exhibit signs of their future path. I know that was true for me.

Before preschool days I used to carry armfuls of my little books around the house in imitation of how the "big kids" went to class. When I began attending kindergarten under the watchful eye of an open-minded teacher, I often finished my lessons quickly and then helped my classmates with theirs.

No surprise, then, that my lifelong mission statement is: "To learn, to love, to teach so that others may have a better life."

Trusting the Inner Voice

The Wise Inner Counselor is always available and speaks to us the most precious words of encouragement we will ever hear—especially when we never cease asking the interior presence, "Who am I?" and "Who are you?"

Looking back I can see that even in my darkest hours I never stopped listening for the voice to answer me. As life unfolded, I turned listening into a spiritual practice that sustained me through a volatile career in theater, a divorce, nearly two decades of living in a spiritual community, the death of both parents, and my career as an instructor.

Being attentive to the wise one's promptings enhanced the eighteen years of marriage I shared with my beloved Stephen, and saw me through the excruciating period of his illness and passing. During the fifteen years since he has been gone, listening has been my lifeline, and the clarity of Love's voice has increased.

Seeking Greater Illumination

My life these days is no longer entirely of this world. My thoughts fly up to Spirit more often than they used to. I find myself seeking greater illumination in order to accomplish the mission I was born to fulfill.

For I know that whatever spiritual progress I make in this life is all I will take with me when that life ends.

Most of all, I know that progress depends on my attunement with the presence that unfailingly leads me through the swells and troughs of the universal voyage into Selfhood that has continued to transcend itself since time immemorial.

Chapter Six

The Perpetual Thread of Contact

When I was a child I wanted to be an archaeologist. I was fascinated by the prospect of uncovering hidden treasures from the ancient civilizations of Egypt, Greece, and Rome—although I was more interested in artifacts of esoteric knowledge and belief than in pottery shards or temple ruins.

Studying transpersonal psychology led me on a different kind of dig that confirmed many guiding principles I had already discovered in wisdom teachings that have been handed down from generations of wise ones since long before the days of ancient Egypt.

Perennial or Perpetual?

In 1945 prolific author, philosopher, and mystic Aldous Huxley revived the term "perennial philosophy" to describe the concept of the individual's potential for direct contact with the Infinite. This idea has surfaced as world-changing revelations in myriad cultures, in every age.[5]

I am convinced that this single understanding of the soul's ability to make personal, unmediated connection with the divine spark in the heart and the Highest Self is the most significant concept in the history of humankind. Despite persistent opposition, this is the idea that has shaped golden ages and inspired the Great Lights of every age to champion the individual's right and freedom to embody the True Self.

Throughout history one reason for the perennial philosophy's apparent disappearance is that great avatars, mystics, and spiritual teachers have been anathematized as heretics, their teachings suppressed or destroyed.

In countless centuries orthodox elites have reduced the soul's pursuit of union with Ultimate Reality to little more than myth or legend.

Nevertheless, although understanding of our innately transcendent nature may have occasionally gone underground, the concept has never entirely vanished. The perennial is really the perpetual. Had the vast library at Alexandria and other repositories of ancient learning survived, we would have abundant examples of wisdom's continuity.

Fortunately, some proof did endure.

During the Middle Ages monastic scribes in Ireland dedicated their lives to the reclamation of antiquity's knowledge. They copied every text they could get their hands on—from the scriptural and philosophical to the mundane.[6]

Wisdom traditions also continued to flourish in Asia and the Middle East. In the eighteenth and nineteenth centuries international trade introduced to the West fragments of Eastern literature that soon burgeoned into an earnest study by poets, writers, and philosophers who were hungry for perspectives that transcended stubbornly embedded strictures of formal religious and social doctrine and dogma.

The Eternal Quest for Meaning

Such hunger has always informed humanity's most influential advocates of the soul's true identity and purpose. Regardless of labels, cultures, or historical challenges to learning, what seekers of every age have tapped into is the perpetual thread of contact that is our lifeline to the source of Being itself.

History's revealed religions have all appeared as attempts to explain the inexplicable—to create pathways of understanding that human minds can comprehend. Here is the eternal quest for meaning, the odyssey toward an infinite destination, the voyage whose purpose is to live an illumined life.

Identifying the Timeless

What is dramatically perpetual is the search for the within. And the within is found when the seeker becomes the seer who knows, at last, the truth of Being as the interior cosmos that has always existed.

The aim of wisdom teachings is to light the traveler's way to the heart of their True Self. Unfortunately, each time an authentic master or avatar has appeared, few adherents have maintained the stream of revelation by assimilating it. Others have interpreted the teacher's insights from a limited perspective that introduces the relativity of the earth-bound self.

Stories that are, at best, an approximation of the truth are spun out of the original release. And because story is more attractive to the human mind than concepts that challenge entrenched habits of thought and behavior, concretized belief systems have accommodated the conditioned self with substitute practices that mimic the soul's real, direct connection with its source.

Once again people become confused or lost until the next revelation of cosmic innovation is released—until a beacon of wholeness shines into their hearts and minds, encouraging them to continue the search for wisdom's thread of contact.

Humanity Needs a Lifeline

Because we dwell in the relativity of time and space, we need a lifeline to the eternal essence that is the most authentic part of ourselves. I am convinced that our task in this century is not only the liberation of our individual souls from inner and outer limitation. We are also responsible for freeing the light of ancient wisdom so it may shine without obstruction.

The perpetual vine of illumination is determined to rise again and again from the soil of humanity's potential. But unless that vine is watered and fertilized with the insights of each successive age, the branch on which future generations are meant to flower will be too weak to sustain them.

Heeding the Voice of Love

We are in need of a direct transmission from the Wise Inner Counselor who is the voice of Love at the core of all that is good and true and beautiful about us. As the presence of these eternal verities, our interior sage creates a vision of luminous realms that raise our soul to heights it knows as real.

Tales of spiritual heroism thrill and inspire us to throw off the shackles of limitation that have beset humanity forever. The freedom to penetrate the underlying mystery of those stories is essential for us to fulfill our reason for being.

This is the common thread known to all of history's Great Lights. When I consider their lives, I discover a synergy that unifies their intentions across the centuries. Each one built on the achievements of their predecessors and in their own way tried to create a good society—an environment in which the authentic Self can flourish.

As potential contributors to the continuity of planetary wisdom and the elimination of ignorance about who we really are, we contact the same ancestral spirit and give voice to its longing to rise within us.

Chapter Seven

Our Heritage of Transcendence

Each of us has sprung from a generational tree that goes back centuries. If we can point to where we came from, we may have a better idea of where we are going, even if that means striking out in a totally different direction from our forebears.

When my father traced the Lafferty family's genealogy to eighteenth-century Ireland, I gained a vivid image of my ancestors. Reading about five intrepid Lafferty brothers who sailed to the American colonies from County Antrim, bought land from William Penn, and fought in the Revolutionary War opened a window into my own pioneering spirit.

Kindled by Our Antecedents

We are also born of a spiritual lineage that we can trace through traditions of faith or philosophy or any field that speaks to us because we intuitively recognize our souls as threads woven into the same tapestry.

Like the master-apprentice tradition of learning a craft from one who embodies the fullness of that profession, the hearts of seekers in every age have been kindled by their antecedents who have acted as steel to their untried flint, sparking the fire of inner knowing about who and what they could be.

Finding Your Spiritual Ancestors

In my conversations with fellow travelers about the path of

self-transcendence, all have agreed that a daunting challenge is connecting with those who will support their way of being in the world. Fortunately, these seekers do tend to recognize each other when they meet, and the Universe often sends enlightened advisers with whom they can identify.

Sometimes those advisers are modern, like the mentors who have dramatically helped shape my life and calling.[7] Others may be historical figures, such as the wise ones who initiated fresh perspectives of soul reality that raised the consciousness of an entire millennium. Or those like William Wordsworth who gave the English language a romantic poetry of individual experience.

Others who have emerged as my transcendent forebears are Ralph Waldo Emerson, who integrated aspects of perennial philosophy into American literature. George W. Russell (Æ), who revived for the Irish their own ancestral spirit. And Dr. Abraham H. Maslow, who developed a positive psychology of Being that revolutionized the field of psychotherapy for decades.

Their Wisdom Is Timeless

These incomparable individuals were beings of exquisite mind and heart. I frequently turn to them as treasured ancestors in my personal genealogy of transcendence.

I find the centuries in which they lived to be irrelevant. Like the adepts who came before and after them, they made contact with the immortal that is imminent in all life. What they revealed about the inner landscape is timeless and applies as equally today as it did to those who knew them, heard the passion in their voices, and thrilled to the revolutionary ideas they espoused.

Trailblazers and Mapmakers

Transcendent greatness shines brightest when awakening others to their own unique gifts. These wayshowers recorded their personal responses to life and held up that mirror of genius to show the rest of us the possibility of achieving our fullest potential.

They felt the fire of destiny that, once kindled, did not let them rest until they had left maps for us to follow on the trails they had blazed.

They worked tirelessly from an immediacy that made them uncommonly attentive to differences between a material world that promised only hindrances of convention and a spiritual world that offered refuge, inspiration, and freedom.

They imbibed the wisdom of the ages and enhanced it through prolific writing and speaking that expanded the boundaries of universal knowledge.

Like their own spiritual forebears, these illumined ones gave voice to their soul's calling and conceived new avenues of understanding. In their own way, each was seeking to enliven dull minds locked in lifeless tradition—to liberate souls imprisoned by the poison of ideological bias that had been taught to them from infancy.

Synthesizing Ancient Wisdom

Great minds are drawn to other great minds. Authors of modern classics study authors of earlier classics. Many act as synthesizers of myriad schools of thought, which is something transcenders often do naturally.

With similar love for the plight of humanity, today's wise ones sharpen their words into rapiers of light to pierce the complacency of sleep-walking generations. Theirs is an enfired partnership that still resounds throughout the ages in the hearts and minds of all who would rise above an unreal self.

Following Our Transcending Forebears

I am fascinated by the transcenders whom I feel called to follow, including my spiritual teacher who raised the perennial wisdom of the Divine Mother to a height of personal actualization in this century.

I love these women and men for their humanity as well as their spirituality. I never tire of reading them. I feel a deep kinship with them and a personal resonance with the paths they forged.

This is the same experience I have when I am attuned to my Wise Inner Counselor. This makes sense to me. As mutual offspring of the Divine, we are one at the level of a higher mind that enlightened individuals have always accessed.

Embracing Our Infinitude

We can synthesize only what we have internalized—what we have become. We take the known into ourselves. We assimilate it. And then we allow the creativity of inner genius to alchemize that understanding into a new facet of Self.

We are changed and so is the knowledge we have imbibed. Knowledge plus love becomes wisdom, and we become wise.

When we pay attention to the Great Lights who have sailed the voyage of self-transcendence before us, we observe the True Self as timeless. When we align with our Wise Inner Counselor who is indelibly connected to Ultimate Reality, we actualize the gifts that only we can express.

Exceeding a limited self requires sacrifices that we are often unwilling to make. Yet when we follow our transcendent ancestors' primary desire for direct spiritual experience, we can discover a deep personal understanding of what Emerson called humanity's "infinitude."

Even when our soul's drive for wholeness challenges us to give up our most cherished habits of perception, we can find our way through the dank waters of unreality.

Psychology Needed Maslow

Of course, the cherished habit of perception that we are most loath to surrender is the one of which we are least aware—our psychology.

The concept of a fully functioning, psychologically healthy human being needed Dr. Maslow to demonstrate the luminous journey to wholeness that he and enlightened transcenders before him perceived as both necessary and possible, if only people would reach deeper, wider, and higher.

Heir to the Perennial

We teach who we are. Shining a psychological light on this understanding is the endeavor that Maslow undertook in articulating the revolutionary way of being he embodied as a vivid example of the self-transcendent qualities he was studying.

If we are searching for an heir to the perennial philosophy's continuity who understands how to make its tenets accessible to secular as well as spiritual audiences, we need look no farther than this much-beloved professor.

"Wordsworth Country"
On the walking trail between Ambleside and Grasmere
The Lake District, Cumbria, England

Chapter Eight

Reflecting on Your Luminous Life - 1

Life can be so busy that time for contemplation may seem too luxurious for daily practice. Yet, as my Wise Inner Counselor has reminded me, we enter into the spacious precincts of self-transcendence through contemplation.

To honor that reminder, I am including a pause in our mutual journey so we may reflect upon where we have been, what "more" we may be discovering, or what thoughts or feelings may be emerging for us.

Enjoy the Pause
Before we delve into the groundbreaking innovations of Dr. Maslow, I invite you to let your imagination flow into that fluid interior space where your Wise Inner Counselor can speak to you of your own luminosity.

You may wish to consider who are your spiritual ancestors. Are there historical figures who have inspired you? Or are there contemporary individuals who exemplify the ideals you most admire? Perhaps there are practices from a cultural or faith tradition that connect you with your own inner wisdom.

If you are inspired to keep a journal or notebook (I like to write on the blank pages of artist sketch pads), you might want to start a section in which to record your experiences as our shared exploration of self-transcendence continues.

A Story of Timeless Intervals

Stephen and I often felt our awareness expanding while reading spiritual literature or the poetry of Wordsworth and Coleridge—the English Romantics who popularized the perennial concept of direct, personal contact with the "inward eye."

We referred to these glimpses of other dimensions as "Wordsworthian" moments—timeless intervals when the poet's vividly descriptive inspirations from the lush Lake District he loved elevated our minds and hearts into the sublime.

Many times a vibration of rich connection with ethereal landscapes would enfold us in a numinous serenity that we felt certain Wordsworth had discovered.

Those moments still occur to me. Often I will feel an *aha!* of insight. Other awakenings bring an awareness of compassion. Some moments emerge as a feeling of warmth, wholeness, or a perception of radiant light. And some are truly ecstatic, enfolding me in a sensation of oneness with the entire Universe.

In whatever form these timeless instants appear, they always change me for the better. This is more than knowledge. These are the deep perceptions of immortality that "see into the life of things."

Embracing the Hidden Richness

As you pause for reflection throughout this book, I encourage you to embrace the hidden richness at the heart of contemplation and the potential insights that can be found in those moments of solitary communion with the inner voice.

There are no "shoulds" or rules in these intervals—only your attunement and the possibility of timeless instants that appear when you offer them the spaciousness of your inner guide who welcomes your attention.

At the Heart of Contemplation

Stop a moment;
abide with me
and learn the secret
of silence and repose.

Look out now across the lake
that glistens in your memory
of still water.

Attend with reverence
majestic eagles holding vigil
in snow-domed radiance,
while noisy ducklings splash and feed
as if this pond were all their own.

Lakes, like dreams,
contain vast motion,
even as they serenely mirror
back to us
imaginings we have
brought them to be shown.

What will you notice
in other moments at the heart
of contemplation?

Dr. Abraham H. Maslow

Part Two

The Need for Transcendence

Inside Maslow's Psychology of Being

*Most human minds believe in splits;
but those once wakened
never tire of sharing miracles
of sweet communion—
the special blend of here and there
that transcends time and space
on a bridge of endless unity.*

Chapter Nine

Why Study Maslow?

Like those who avidly read the books of Abraham H. Maslow when his landmark theories were first published, I study him because he explains me to myself.

I get the sense that he may have experienced the same self-validation when he discovered his own thoughts, feelings, and psychological ventures being reported to him by the remarkable people who were the subjects of his inquiry.

Maslow is quick to emphasize that his portrayal of the top qualities of psychologically healthy individuals is a composite. Not everyone reports or exhibits every feature. Still, while studying the results of his lifetime of research, I have found a clearer, more vivid image of the kind of person I strive to be.

Understanding Maslow's Terminology

Finding the right words to describe his innovative ideas was one of the challenges Maslow confronted in developing his theories. So, he coined new words. The familiar terms of self-actualization, self-transcendence, and peak experience are part of the lexicon he evolved. He also used familiar words in unfamiliar ways.

Throughout his career he continued to refine his definitions of the terms that ultimately could only approximate his meaning. He seems to have inhabited a spherical world that complicated the task of conveying his concepts in the linear, scientific language of existing psychological studies.

Maslow does his best to help us understand what he is observing and experiencing. But do we really get it? Or rather than opening our minds to the unique perspectives he is sharing, do we make assumptions based on what we think a word means?

Avoiding Concrete Thinking

As I have delved into Maslow's vast body of work, I have noticed a tendency in my own thinking to concretize his ideas into definitions that are more mentally accessible.

This desire of my linear mind to settle for the familiar is not effective with Maslow. His concepts are often very subtle. His deeper meanings can easily be missed if I do not apply my own inner wisdom to meet him where he is.

I am convinced that offering my Wise Inner Counselor the opportunity to quicken my intuition is a vital key to unlocking the depths of Maslovian psychology.

The Heart of Maslow's Work

In late 1966 Maslow was on the cusp of his realization that self-transcendence emerges at the top of his Hierarchy of Human Needs. In a letter to Henry Geiger (the person whom he believed was one of the few to understand his work in depth), he mentions an article in which his colleague refers to Emerson as someone who trusted his judgments and intuitions, and whom history had shown to be correct in doing so.

In that article Geiger had asked, "How does one get to become an Emerson?" He might as easily have pondered how one becomes a Wordsworth or an Æ. Or he could have asked, "How does one become a Maslow?"

The professor answered that the question was broader than one great mind. Rather, each individual must ask how he or she can become "a sure person, one who has authentic inner voices and who hears them and has courage to act on them."[8]

Here is the heart of Maslow's work and the secret of how he became who he was—and how Wordsworth, Emerson, and Æ did the same. They observed themselves. They paid attention to their intuition. They acted on what they were perceiving to create the unique legacies they left for those who would follow them.

And every one of them, including Maslow, read literature from the East.

The Essential Question

One of my favorite ideas from Maslow is to focus on what he called the "matter-in-hand." In other words, what is the issue that attracts your keenest attention? At the moment, I am drawn to ask an essential question:

> What do we who desire to transcend the limited self really need to know about the psychology of Being in order to create a luminous life?

The following chapters in this section are my attempt to answer that question by exploring the core concepts of Maslow's multiple innovations that have been most useful to my personal exploration of self-transcendence.

Chapter Ten

Maslow the Transcender

American writer and philosopher Henry Geiger[9] wrote that Maslow must "first be thought of as a man, and then as one who worked very hard at psychology."[10] He said that the professor's integration of his personal evolution as a man is what created a new way of thinking about psychology.

Dr. Warren Bennis[11] agreed. In his eulogy delivered two days after Maslow's death, he explained: "I quote lavishly from Abe's own work, because his work is his life, and to know one is to greet the other."[12]

Absorbing Maslow

To truly fathom Maslow's perspective requires entering into the transcendence he achieved. Though he rarely cites his own ecstatic experiences in the exalted dimensions he called "peaks," for many years he had been doing far more than studying what others reported. He was living transcendently.

Comprehending him becomes a matter of assimilation, of imbibing the essence of his wisdom, of allowing a transmission of his holistic thinking to infuse us as we read him.

We may catch glimpses of Maslow the transcender by looking up at him from the bottom of his hierarchy. But to fully engage him, we do as he did. We forsake limitation and step into the realm of illumined consciousness he inhabited with his Wise Inner Counselor, into his deep compassion for the entire dynamic scope of human nature. Through this holistic perspective, we unite with his conviction that every person is "the most beautiful, the most sacred, the most perfect in the world."[13]

In Perpetual Transition

Dr. Maslow appears to have been in perpetual transition from one innovation to another. He seemed to be living, speaking, and writing in the spaces between his most recent idea and the next concept that would emerge from his penetrating observations.

In the revealing interview that he and Warren Bennis videotaped in 1968, he explained that he always wrote with his yet-unborn, great-great-grandchildren in mind. He envisioned a future that would support those children's freedom to become their most complete selves.

When a sudden, fatal heart attack tipped him into that future on June 8, 1970, it became the task of others to share the nectar of love and wisdom they had absorbed from the humble man they knew as "Abe."

In Memoriam

On October 25, 1970 a memorial service was held by Maslow's friends and colleagues from Brandeis University, where he had established the school's first psychology department.

The reminiscences were poignant, as those who knew him well came to grips with the fact that this treasured person, who had been so vibrant in the exuberant, childlike wonder with which he lived, was no longer walking among them.

They chronicled his groundbreaking achievements—not the least of which had been giving the field of psychology a new language in the abundance of terms he coined to describe the answers he was formulating for the revolutionary questions he had been raising for decades.

His friends talked about his relentless battle with an atomistic, mechanistic, valueless mindset that he said plagued the sciences and that turned many religions into doctrines that opposed direct, unmediated, personal spiritual experience.

Abe's associates remembered him as loving, honest, loyal, and generous with an easy sense of humor and an openness to the full expression of his own potential as a human being.

They vividly recalled how they had been touched by the inner force that kept him sailing into the rarefied air of the Unknown. His flashes of insight often surprised them (and him) by spinning out fresh perspectives that integrated profound ancient wisdom with modern science.

One of the most insightful recollections is from his close friend Ricardo B. Morant who described how Maslow searched for a name for his unique view of human nature. Now that he had passed, his work was being referred to as Maslovian psychology.

Dr. Morant quipped that "were [Abe] still alive, the title of his next book surely would be *Beyond Maslovian Psychology*."[14]

The Professor's Path

Henry Geiger had once characterized his friend as a "philosopher of science."[15] Those words are not often combined. I wanted to understand what Geiger meant.

I knew that Maslow had continued to transcend his graduate work in behaviorism and his later exploration of Freudian psychoanalysis. He had helped found psychology's humanistic "third force" and eventually published his observations of the farther reaches of human nature as the necessary "fourth force" that he called Transpersonal Psychology.[16]

A New Breed

Although poets, saints, and sages have been living the principles of transcendence throughout history and teaching them in every age, Maslow was the first to explicitly articulate the characteristics of a fully functioning, psychologically healthy human being in a modern, secular context.

He called himself a "new breed—a theoretical psychologist"[17] who considered himself a scientist. Yet he was also highly intuitive and commented that he often was not sure where his ideas came from.

Although he was an accomplished researcher, Maslow tended to present his innovative theories in broad strokes so that others might do further research and conduct experiments to support and expand his ideas. From reading his notes and articles, I sense that he realized, perhaps only subconsciously, that he had but a short time in which to establish the study and practice of psychology within its fourth force.

He trusted the illuminations that occurred to him and maintained a lifelong enthusiasm for what was novel, creative, fresh, and unusual. His books and lectures reflect his belief that human nature is basically good and that his job as a psychologist was to "find that germ of goodness, describe it, and show us how it should be developed."[18]

During his second year in college he experienced a revelation that his mission in this life was to use his intelligence to combat irrationality and create a better world. Not long after that he discovered behaviorism and set off to immerse himself in this provocative science—which he later transcended.

Child as Father of the Man

Abraham Harold Maslow was born on April 1, 1908 in Manhattan,

New York, to parents who had fled Russia in one of the great waves of European immigration in the early twentieth century. Abe was their eldest child.

His father was a barrel-maker who worked long hours away from home to make a success of his business and possibly to avoid the difficult personality of his wife. As a result, the father gave little nurturing attention to his first-born. In a way, young Abe raised himself.

Although he grew up in a large extended family, Maslow remembered his childhood as miserable, due in large part to the cruelty he experienced from his mother—a narrow-minded woman whose superstitions tainted her son's concept of religion.

Very early in life, young Abe found solace in the local library where he earned an adult library card, because he had read every book in the children's section.

He was a highly intelligent, though gawky lad who suffered from extremely low self-esteem and abuse from gangs that roamed his neighborhood. Fortunately, his life changed once he entered high school and then attended college.

There he found the intellectual climate that propelled him along the academic ascent that gave him contact with many of the eminent psychologists, psychiatrists, and anthropologists of the 1930s and 1940s.

Developing His Signature Theory

During those years Maslow befriended and studied with many prominent scholars who had escaped persecution in Europe and settled in New York City. It was this abundance of brilliant and stimulating mentors that inspired him to synthesize the existing major fields of psychotherapy into his revolutionary theory of human motivation, known as the Hierarchy of Human Needs.

Yet Maslow remained an outsider. He did not permanently attach himself to any one school of thought or practice. In fact, throughout his career he was accused by many colleagues of being anti-science, when what he actually was trying to do was open up science to the values of human experience.

As he navigated his career on the roller coaster of worldwide conflicts and wars, economic depression, and pervasive ethnic prejudice, Maslow became intent on developing what he called "a psychology for the peace table."

His primary desire was to foster increased mental health in large numbers of people who would create a free society to support the continued development of its citizens.[19]

Self-Actualization Needs
Seeks fulfillment
of personal potential

Esteem Needs
Seeks esteem through recognition
or achievement of group
or personal goals

Belonging Needs
Seeks to receive & give affection;
affiliation with like-minded groups

Safety Needs
Seeks security through protection,
security, order, law, limits, stability

Survival Needs
Seeks to obtain the basic necessities of life:
air, food, drink, shelter, sleep

Figure 1
Maslow's Original Theory of Human Motivation
(Hierarchy of Human Needs)
showing Deficiency-needs in the order in which
most people experience them.

Chapter Eleven

Essentials of Motivation

From the beginning of his career, Maslow knew that he had set himself a daunting task. He admits that anyone who attempts a holistic approach to the complexities of human motivation faces major challenges.

Still, he persevered, because he was convinced in the way a natural transcender knows in his bones that what *ought* to be actually *is* when you have the courage to study the highest potentials achieved by the most remarkable people.

As Maslow began to synthesize his contemporaries' psychological, philosophical, scientific, and theological perceptions of what it means to be a complete, fully realized human, he ran into entrenched dichotomies. Where others saw only parts, he saw unity, or what *could* be a unity of these various disciplines.

His original Theory of Human Motivation presented the human psyche in terms of a unified system in which what happens to one part affects the whole.

The Potency of Deficiency-Needs

Maslow proposed that individuals need what they most acutely lack. The basic requirements for human life form a hierarchy of what he called "Deficiency-needs," which appear in most people in the order of physical survival, safety, belonging, esteem, and self-actualization.

When a Deficiency-need is satisfied, it disappears from a

person's awareness, and the next higher-order need dominates their consciousness until it is satisfied. And so, on up the hierarchy.

Problems with the Pyramid Symbol

Although the five-tiered pyramid has become an iconic symbol for Maslow's original hierarchy of needs, he identifies his model as a synthesis that may be called a "general-dynamic" theory.

He says that his theory is not nearly as rigid as some might think (and as the pyramid graphic suggests). He makes the point that previously satisfied needs may reemerge if they are thwarted. In addition, individuals who have consistently experienced fulfillment of a certain need are apt to withstand its deprivation in the future.

Although most people do seem to have these needs in this order, there are exceptions—such as those for whom self-esteem is more important than love. Or those whose drive for creativeness is stronger than any other motivation.

Maslow is never fixed in his perspectives. Even in this first proposal of a new approach to human motivation, he seems to be in motion. He affirms the accuracy of his model while including language that broadens interpretation of the hierarchy of needs—subject to his evolving observations.

Unsatisfied Basic Needs

Maslow asserted that each of us harbors an innate human nature of vast potential that becomes blocked or thwarted through deprivation of lower needs. He was convinced that self-actualization was rare, because most adults were still trying to satisfy unmet Deficiency-needs.

He observed that many human behaviors are not the result of psychological illness. Rather, they are simply the best people are capable of doing in their attempts to satisfy needs of which they may not be consciously aware.

He said that our most basic needs are meant to be fulfilled in the first years of life. The fact that they are not met for a significant number of people means that we have large populations of wounded inner children walking around in adult bodies trying to figure out why they feel like part of their identity is missing.

Some Self-Actualizers Are Different

Maslow had initially included self-actualization in Deficiency-needs. However, his subsequent research revealed differences in many individuals who were consciously striving to realize their full potential. Their way of being in the world was not the same as those who merely lived to satisfy their basic human needs.

The individuals in this group were psychologically mature and grounded. As well as their being dedicated to achieving excellence and success in their chosen fields, Maslow found them to be universally committed to some vocation or cause greater than themselves. They took more pleasure in many interests with less fear, anxiety, or boredom than those who were still dealing with Deficiency-needs.

These self-actualizers revealed a general love of life. They were very accepting of themselves, fascinated by the unknown, naturally spontaneous, highly creative, and tended toward a childlike ability to repeatedly appreciate the same experience.

Maslow's advanced self-actualizers had a strong sense of personal autonomy that allowed them to be solitary with greater ease than others. In their thinking they were strongly independent. As self-starters they were growth-motivated and resistant to the conventions of their cultures.

One of Those Challenging Terms

Maslow identified self-actualizers as being more objective than the average person, which he said made them "problem-centered rather than ego-centered."

I would like to use a different term here. From my perspective, calling self-actualizers problem-centered sounds like they are focused on what is wrong with life rather than perceiving the holistic worldview that Maslow ascribed to them.

I believe what he really meant is that self-actualizers are likely to be fact-seekers who view the matter-in-hand with less ego-bias than others. If an actual problem exists, they aim for solutions that benefit all parties involved rather than merely satisfying their own personal agendas.

My Observation of Self-Esteem

As I have worked with Maslow's theory of human motivation in my various occupations as personal development instructor, life coach, and retreat leader, I have become aware of a dynamic that can occur within people who are striving to fulfill their reason for being.

When someone's self-esteem is largely dependent upon satisfying belonging needs, they may lack a vigorous resiliency when the group to which they belong is challenged. Or when they are opposed by other members of their group.

Conversely, those who are increasing their reliance on the inner voice of wisdom become independent of peer pressure and begin to act from a deeper sense of honor for the True Self.

I am convinced that achieving the self-actualization that Maslow defined as "the full use and exploitation of talents, capacities, potentialities, etc.,"[20] is not possible as long as one is tied to the opinions of others.

The growth of healthy Self-esteem is not the result of merely satisfying a lack. It is a way of life that only increases to new levels of potency as we pay attention to our Wise Inner Counselor.

Identifying Two Types of Self-Actualizers

Eventually, Maslow began to differentiate between two types of self-actualizers. The first type were psychologically healthy but showed little or no interest in growing beyond the fulfillment of their personal talents. The second type were those for whom the transcendent aspects of life were important, even central.

In other words, some individuals did tend to approach self-actualization as a Deficiency-need. As long as they were doing what they believed they were born for, they were content—and likely highly competent. However, they felt no need for the ecstatic episodes of peak experiences in which the higher-motivated actualizers eagerly engaged.

Maslow soon identified "peakers" and "non-peakers" as exhibiting distinct and significant differences. This really was a watershed realization for him that quickly led to his theory of self-transcendence.

My sense is that finally coming to the conclusion that some of his subjects thought and used language akin to religious people may also have inspired him to more fully embrace those aspects of his own psychology.

Peak Experiences and Other Phenomena

Maslow theorized that all people have some form of peak experience or moments of highest happiness and fulfillment. However, societal pressure, education, and cultural or faith traditions can cause us to discount or forget that we have been touched by the sublime more often than we remember.

The professor often asked his students to record examples of any such experiences they could recall, even if they were brief *aha!* moments of intuitive inspiration. When they began to identify and accept the presence of peak experiences in their lives, many of the students started to change.

As they gained awareness of their capacity to enter into more refined states of consciousness, lesser wants and desires began to fall away and altruistic values began to take precedence.

Maslow also observed that interferences with the ability of the genuine "peakers" to continue their quest for the transcendental sometimes resulted in their developing psychological disturbances such as depression, boredom, or a lost of zest for life. He called these anomalies "metapathologies."[21]

Psychology of Inner Wisdom

When Maslow presented his theory of Being-psychology, he was articulating what I am convinced is the psychology of the Wise Inner Counselor. When he describes the fulfillment and joy one experiences while actually living in "Being-cognition,"[22] he is articulating the felt sense of living in attunement with inner wisdom.

This is the state of self-transcendence—of going beyond deficiency oriented self-actualization and reaching for the stars of our spiritual potential where we perceive the wholeness and universality of our Selfhood.

Beginning with Love in Mind

I was excited to learn that Maslow's revolutionary theory of Being-cognition emerged from a study of love relationships in self-actualizing individuals and then of other people.

He discovered that love centered around Deficiency-needs

tends to be self-serving and egoic. Conversely, he observed Being-love as selfless, non-interfering, and able to perceive qualities in the beloved that a selfish lover cannot detect.

This makes me think of the loving relationships so many of us have with our pets. Domestic animals have an ability to evoke in us humans the spontaneous affection that we may have trouble offering to others or to ourselves.

How many times have you heard someone say that the sweet animal they rescued actually rescued them? This is the kind of non-judgmental love that Maslow observed in his fully human self-actualizers.

He writes that his previous training as a psychologist did not prepare him for this discovery. Instead, he found vivid descriptions of Being-love in the literatures of mysticism, art, creativeness, and religion. He was even reminded of Emerson's transcendental idealism that conceived of the Universe as a unit in which humans are vitally and lovingly included.[23]

By focusing on Being-love, I am convinced that Maslow firmly established his psychology of Being in the all-pervading cosmic consciousness of the Wise Inner Counselor who always begins with the presence of "capital L" Love in mind.

Abraham H. Maslow (left) with author Frank Goble (right)
Historical photo from 1970

Chapter Twelve

At the Heart of Maslow

Dr. Maslow must have been a delightful professor. He is described as being warm, witty, gregarious, and generous with his time. He seemed to have had a great capacity to love. Although he concentrated on researching, writing, and teaching, he made himself available to counsel students in his home or office, though not in a clinical setting.

Those conversations helped many young people navigate their difficult college years. These gatherings also gave Maslow an opportunity to explore in a relaxed and friendly atmosphere the trajectory of human potential from deficiencies to beingness in those students who fondly called their popular professor "the Frank Sinatra of Brooklyn College."[24]

Exploring Higher Possibilities

As Maslow's theories gained acceptance later in his career, he became a highly sought-after lecturer and consultant.

One of his more significant theories, which was welcomed by some in the entrepreneurial business world, was what he called *Eupsychia*—the good society or good company that creates conditions in which the essential needs of its members are met and a general condition of psychological health prevails.

He often speculated on what type of society one thousand self-actualizing people might create if they were left alone to function together without interference.

For most of his career, Maslow focused on what he called "the higher possibilities" of humanity. He wanted to know how far people could develop when they were permitted to do so.

He clearly understood that we must have achieved a firm sense of our identity before we can transcend it. We do not soar to great heights of self-mastery until we have grown psychological wings strong enough to handle the mighty winds of life that will surely test our mettle when we attempt to live in the refined dimensions of higher consciousness.

The Search for Meaning

In the initial publication of his theory of human motivation, Maslow devoted multiple paragraphs to the need "to understand, to systematize, to organize, to analyze, to look for relations and meanings."[25] He noticed how these needs seem to arrange themselves into a small hierarchy that begins with a desire to know.

My sense is that he was describing the presence of the Wise Inner Counselor who pervades individual consciousness, encourages psychological growth toward higher motivations, and offers insights that lead to problem-solving at every level of human need.[26]

Maslow found this tendency to be especially prevalent in his most psychologically grounded self-transcenders.

Insights Ahead of His Time

Throughout his life Maslow retained a profound respect for animals as well as humans. Whether he was studying monkeys, dogs, or people, he beheld his subjects with genuine affection and his full attention. In that concentrated state, he discovered the deepest motivations, hopes, dreams, and potentials of the farther frontiers of human nature.

Maslow's work constituted the first time that the values, virtues, and consciousness of healthy, inwardly attuned persons was addressed by psychology, rather than by philosophy or religion. His research led him into areas of the human psyche that no psychologist or psychiatrist had penetrated with such clear perception, with such appreciation for what he was observing, or with such a concurrent ability to articulate that perception.

Only toward the end of his life did many of his academic colleagues acknowledge the importance of his contribution to psychology. Others in the fields of philosophy and education also were slow to catch up with him.

Even today few teach his expanded theory of self-transcendence, preferring instead to focus on the more familiar study of self-actualization. Maslow demonstrated in his own life that in order to perceive transcendence you need to be transcending. Not everyone chooses to do so.

Nature or Nurture?

I am convinced that mystics and others who persist in transcending their life circumstances are born with that soul urge—at least latently within them. We do not enter this life as a *tabula rasa* (a blank tablet).

From the time Maslow was four years old, he was testing the validity of his mother's superstitions. His siblings showed no such proclivity, which was one reason why he felt like an oddball in his family.

Later, when he was intensely involved in various fields of psychology, he persistently transcended the conventional thinking to which many in those fields were committed. Instead, he synthesized new approaches to existing ideas and formulated entirely original theories.

Maslow was convinced that individuals could become more transcendent when they were made aware of their own peak experiences. And he did have some success in moving people out of Deficiency-needs into clearer contact with the values and awareness of Being-cognition.

Kindling Personal Revelation

Achieving a luminous life often begins with a kindling of what already exists within. That ignition of our innate reality may come in the form of an encounter with a person or concept that sparks a revelation in our thinking and a revolution in our world.

Even natural self-transcenders go through episodes when their lives are turned upside down so they can perceive the next big leap their mission in life is calling them to make.

Maslow talks about his difficulties in exploring the highest reaches of human nature. He says his discoveries involved:

> ...continuous destruction of cherished axioms, the perpetual coping with seeming paradoxes, contradictions and vagueness and the occasional collapse around my ears of long established, firmly believed in and seemingly unassailable laws of psychology.[27]

Always in Process

My own life has been like that. Sometimes I feel like I am doing more unlearning than learning. The more closely I am attuned to my Wise Inner Counselor, the more that concepts of limitation I have held for many years fall away. Thankfully, once they do, a finer perception takes place in my consciousness.

Actualizing our innate potential is a lifelong, evolutionary adventure. Although we may attain stages of personal development that are profoundly fulfilling and where we may abide for a period of time, Maslow observed that even healthy self-actualizers who show little or no preference for peak experiences still continue to learn and grow.

Transcenders who consistently replace previous insights with fresh learning often find themselves entering profoundly transformative realms of Being that are perpetually in motion.

Recognizing Soul Longing

For the transcenders Maslow called "my people," fulfilling the potential of their talents was not the whole story. They reported a greater need for satisfying the deepest longings of their souls.

Maslow also contacted that longing in himself. He came to recognize a certain "godliness" (his term) in those who avidly pursued a way of being in which peak experiences gave them a taste of the Eternal that changed their lives forever.

If Only They Would Try

A lack of this genuine soul motivation presented Maslow with an attitude for which he had little patience.

Because he was so driven to fulfill his own reason for being and because he continued to discover ever deeper and higher potentials in society as well as in individuals, when faced with students who were content with mediocrity, he challenged them.

He observed how the greater affluence that followed World War II, coupled with the mind-numbing influence of television, was actually deteriorating soul-sensitivity in the young.

I think this was one of the behaviors he found most difficult to reconcile with what he felt so passionately to be the hope of the future—if only people would seize the opportunity to be as great as he knew they could be.

The Soul's Place in Psychology

For decades Western psychology seems to have willfully ignored the meaning of "psyche," which is "soul"—focusing instead on illnesses of cognition and behavior in the mental and physiological dimensions of existence. Or reducing transcendent soul experiences to mental aberrations.

Whether or not the term is used, transcendence touches the soul. Maslow was adamant that psychology must include the inner experiences that make life meaningful. Toward the end of his life, he spoke of those personal experiences as creating a stable state of consciousness that he realized signified his own growing mysticism, which life had finally and fully revealed to him.

Others recognized that same mystical quality in him. After his death, tributes like this poured in:

"There was something otherworldly [about Maslow]. He could have talked to Plato or Spinoza with ease, but would have felt just as elated in conversing with a janitor about the virtues of grandchildren."

"It felt good to be human in his presence. In a disturbed world, he saw light and promise and hope and he shared these with the rest of us."[28]

Following His Own Star

In a way, Abraham Maslow's life was his masterpiece. He left his groundbreaking legacy by following the star of his own inner teacher. He was a man with a mission who never stopped learning and growing and surrounding himself with those who also were striving to live a fully human existence.

His life truly was luminous.

Chapter Thirteen

The Way of Love Knowledge

Early in his career Maslow was encouraged by his friend and mentor Max Wertheimer to read literature from the East. He was especially fond of the philosophy of Taoism.

Here Maslow was tapping into a stream of the perennial philosophy that resonated with what he had always known, perhaps only subconsciously. My sense is that this encounter was for him one of those flashes of recognition that ignited a previously unrealized inner awareness.

When referencing Eastern literature, Maslow often used terms relating to concepts that had caught his attention, but his interpretations were uniquely his own.

Always the Synthesizer

I want to make the point here that Maslow always maintained his independence of thought. He was the quintessential synthesizer, which meant that he did not merely borrow bits of established knowledge.

When he detected an element of the perennial in a thought system, he would ferret out the essence of that idea. He would observe it, work it over, and emerge with a novel perception of that concept—usually within the context of a revolutionary theory that elevated the study and practice of psychology to the next level.

In many ways, Maslow's theories represent a synthesis of

Eastern and Western philosophy and science. He integrated the insights of a wide range of illumined texts through the lens of what became transpersonal psychology.

This could be one reason why even his closest colleagues were challenged to keep up with his spherical perception of his subjects and the rapidity with which his theories about them emerged.

The Challenge of Description

From his eclectic perspective, Maslow saw deeply into the values and soul qualities of the people he was observing. He never stopped trying to describe what he was detecting while encouraging his "peakers" in their attempts to become the fullness of what they also were seeing in their own ethereal experiences.

I think Maslow must have realized that a direct approach would never fully articulate the inexpressible characteristics of the Being-realm—which is where I see the perennial philosophy originating.

So, he circled around the limitations of language by approaching from multiple directions the concepts he could see so clearly. In an attempt to make the implicit more succinctly explicit, he was continually refining his theories in books and lectures, adding or clarifying descriptions.

He was like a lighthouse, beaming out fervent transmissions to the self-transcenders that he sensed were out there, just waiting for somebody to explain them to themselves.

Practicing Love Knowledge

When Maslow hit upon the most effective approach to working with people as non-intruding and non-controlling, he must have known that he had struck gold. He was convinced that what he described as non-interfering observation was far more effective than the controlling manipulation he found in other fields of psychotherapy.

One of the most important ways in which Maslow explained this open, receptive approach was to say, "If you love someone, you let them be." Meaning that you let them be who they are meant to be.

He proposed to psychologists, teachers, and parents the practice that he called "love knowledge" or "loving perception."[29] What he meant is that engagement done with your full attention in a mode of receptive objectivity is likely to be more accurate because the observer is inclined to offer positive verbal and non-verbal feedback to the person being observed.

This appreciative approach allows individuals to relax their defenses and let themselves be seen physically, spiritually, and psychologically. My experience is that authentic, heart-to-heart interaction at the level of the Wise Inner Counselor is the result.

Any of us may follow this example of being profoundly engaged with another person without trying to mold them into our preconceived idea. Our interest becomes solely that of their evolutionary progress in life.

The More You Know, the More You Love
I had occasion to experience the benefits of Maslow's love knowledge during the opening weekend sessions of the nine-month course I attended on facilitator training.

There were over a dozen participants plus two main facilitators who conducted some novel get-acquainted activities with the group. The most effective exercise was their invitation for each of us to share the story of our life.

This was no mere "give us the main points" kind of storytelling. If someone needed an hour or more to recount the history of this lifetime, they got it. The level of genuine receptivity in the room was palpable and consistent for every person—no matter if they shared a little or a lot.

Laughter, tears, hugs, and gracious acknowledgement of the courage required to disclose often painful or embarrassing episodes flowed between hearts that opened wide to receive what was being offered. The atmosphere radiated a holiness that felt as if we were being cleansed and sanctified by our confessions.

Loving the Knowledge Gained

The level of intimacy our group reached in this single weekend was astonishing. Not only for what we learned about each other, but also for what we learned about ourselves.

Each person's story became my story. My story became theirs. And in the telling, a third narrative formed. This story told of our group's mutual trust that would carry us through nine months of very challenging psychological work.

If we did not already understand the concept of holding space for another person, we learned it in those initial two days. The truth that was revealed built a level of compassion that I have experienced in few other situations in my life. Certainly not in such a short time.

Looking back on how the first weekend and subsequent sessions of facilitator training unfolded, I can see the activating principle that brought the group together was the presence of each person's authentic Self. Love knowledge is the way that inner guidance works. The more we come to know our Wise Inner Counselor, the more we love that presence. And the more we realize how intensely and persistently we are loved.

Chapter Fourteen

Living in Being-Cognition

In his introduction to *The Farthest Reaches of Human Nature* Henry Geiger says, "the core of what Maslow found out about psychology he found out from himself."[30] The only way he could have identified the heights of consciousness that he perceived in his subjects and then articulated with such immediacy was to be living at that height.

Takes One to Know One
Maslow studied himself with remarkable objectivity—with the idea that "knowledge of one's own deep nature is also simultaneously knowledge of human nature in general."

It takes incredible discipline to continue asking yourself the hard questions that others cannot or will not ask. Until the end of his life, Maslow demonstrated unwavering dedication to his mission, remaining an outsider and not succumbing to the siren song of intellectual or professional comfortability or hubris.

Being Clear About Transcendence
Maslow's research continued to prove his observations that not all self-actualizers had peak experiences or were interested in having them. Whereas for self-transcenders, mystical, sacred, or ecstatic experiences and the lasting insights they evoked were of primary importance.

Interestingly, he found that some people who were not

very mature psychologically and were not self-actualizing also had occasional transcendent experiences. However, they did not appear to be significantly changed in attitude or behavior, nor were they moved to greater psychological balance.

Another nuance that Maslow noticed was that the peak experiences of transcenders tended toward a more spiritual or religious theme than those of merely healthy self-actualizers. Although feelings of awe accompanied both, the context was often different between the two groups.

The peak experiences that self-transcenders reported to Maslow nearly always contained a noetic or cognitive element that informed and often transformed their lives. One reason they welcomed these events was that they were lifelong learners. Many times a peak experience would act as a slingshot to propel them to greater depths of self-awareness and heights of consciousness.

Discoveries of Beingness

Maslow's term for the state of awareness that emerged during peak experiences was "Being-cognition"—a unitive state in which feelings of duality and separateness disappear and the "peaker" contacts timeless, spaceless, eternal existence.

As his work with peak experiences progressed, he recognized that specific values emerge from Being-cognition. These "Being-values" also act as Being-needs or "metaneeds," that are inner drives he called "metamotivations."

His conversations with "peakers" revealed that the values of Being are not hierarchical. To those who reported them, none was more important than the other. It became clear to Maslow that these values are intrinsic and irreducible (like prime numbers) and can be defined in terms of each other.

Characteristics of Self-Transcenders

In addition to the importance which self-transcenders placed on their peak experiences, Maslow wrote extensively about other significant differences he observed in them.

He described them as easily speaking what he called "the language of Being"—the language of mystics, poets, seers, and the deeply religious. Transcenders are more responsive to beauty than non-peaking self-actualizers and are consciously metamotivated by the values of Being.

He talked about transcenders perceiving the sacred within the secular while at the same time being able to handle the more mundane requirements of Deficiency-needs. He appeared to have been very much like that.

Not surprisingly, Maslow said that transcenders tend to recognize each other. He proved that in his own recognition of this unique group. His self-transcending students, colleagues, and a number of associates in the corporate world accepted him as one of their own.

The idea of interpersonal synergy and non-competitiveness became a hallmark of Maslow's approach to management, which he observed in some forward-thinking entrepreneurs who were practicing his theories in their companies. He found these business leaders to be as motivated by the Being-values as were their peers in other professions.

Over the years he noted a high decree of creativeness and innovative spirit in all of the transcenders he met, no matter what occupations they pursued.

Seeing with the Eyes of the True Self

A characteristic that Maslow identified in self-actualizers was their ability to see the world more realistically than others. He found this trait to be even stronger in self-transcenders.

Although peak experiences and the resulting serenity that he termed the "plateau experience" are of prime importance to the self-transcenders, they are not wild-eyed mystics who never come down to earth. Rather, he found them to be eminently practical, grounded, and more willing to face facts than their less psychologically mature associates.

In other words, self-transcenders are able to live with the awe of mystery and still keep their considerable wits about them.

This makes perfect sense to me. If transcending the egoic self in favor of higher states of consciousness and more refined stages of development is actually a function of inner guidance, then the Wise Inner Counselor's clear perception of the way things are would naturally follow.

Values as Ideals

When we observe the Being-values that Maslow and his transcenders considered intrinsic to the human psyche, we approach the territory of idealism—the attempt to live in accordance with the simplest, most fundamental ideals that exist within humanity.

Incidentally, idealism is the term that Emerson used to define Transcendentalism.

To me, metavalues represent the essence of the True Self. There is an ineffable quality to these values that makes them hard to describe. I have found that they can only be fully understood in the felt sense of unitive consciousness that pervades peak experiences and that is transmitted to us by our Wise Inner Counselor in those sublime, revelatory moments of insight that seem to come from afar.

Although Maslow listed more than a dozen Being-values that were most commonly cited by his research subjects, truth, beauty, and goodness were often mentioned as three irreducible values that flow through us as expressions of divine Love.

Perhaps not surprisingly, the True, the Good, and the Beautiful were known in medieval times as "the Transcendentals." They also are called "eternal verities" or "Platonic essences."

In the relativity of modern society, definitions of truth, beauty, and goodness take on many guises. From the viewpoint of the True Self, the intrinsic values are consistent. Here is my attempt to express that perspective:

- The True is the wisdom of inner knowing that comes to us from the Higher Mind.
- The Beautiful is the ineffable perfection of substance and form that pervades divine creativeness.
- The Good is the outpicturing of the other intrinsic values in alignment with the will of our Highest Self.[31]

The Dynamic of Values

I have noticed that values produce action—consistent patterns of behavior, thoughts, feelings, and deeds that provide a window into the soul's individuality. Your soul. My soul. The snowflake pattern or blueprint that defines any given soul.

Each of us contains a core value that Maslow would call our highest metamotivation. That core value may resonate synergistically with a few others. Together they form the scaffolding for our soul growth. And they provide the inner impetus for our pursuit of the unitive way of living that is self-transcendent.

Values to Virtues

The eternal verities of core values have a special function within what we can visualize as a spiral of Being. As these values emerge from peak experiences, we may detect them in the afterglow that heightens our awareness of the mystical landscape that surrounds us, even in everyday life.

Although the otherworldly episodes of peak experiences tend to defy description, we may be able to discuss the values we notice percolating through us with a tangible, felt sense. My experience is that it can be useful to articulate several values, to sit with them and allow our core value to rise to the top like cream in a bottle of unpasteurized milk.

I spent many hours in contemplation before I could identify my core value as wisdom. I sat with it, wrote about it,[32] and watched for ways in which it was appearing in my life. After a while I stopped noticing. Only recently have I realized why.

Values can be likened to mental constructs. Virtues are spiritual essences. In the same way that Deficiency-needs disappear when they are satisfied, when we have assimilated a core value, it disappears as a separate element of personality that we can point to or discuss. It has become a virtue that is now an inextricable part of our being.

Beyond Cognition

A value that has been transformed into a virtue is the ocean in which we swim. It transcends mental constructs. It permeates every realm of consciousness and informs every aspect of our life because we are one with that essence.

Virtue glows. It emanates from us as a soul-fragrance of which we probably are not aware, although others may easily perceive it in us.

When we remark that a person has a certain positive spirit, what we mean is that they radiate a virtue that is a unique expression of their Wise Inner Counselor who lives in the wholeness of Being-consciousness where we are meant to be most at home.

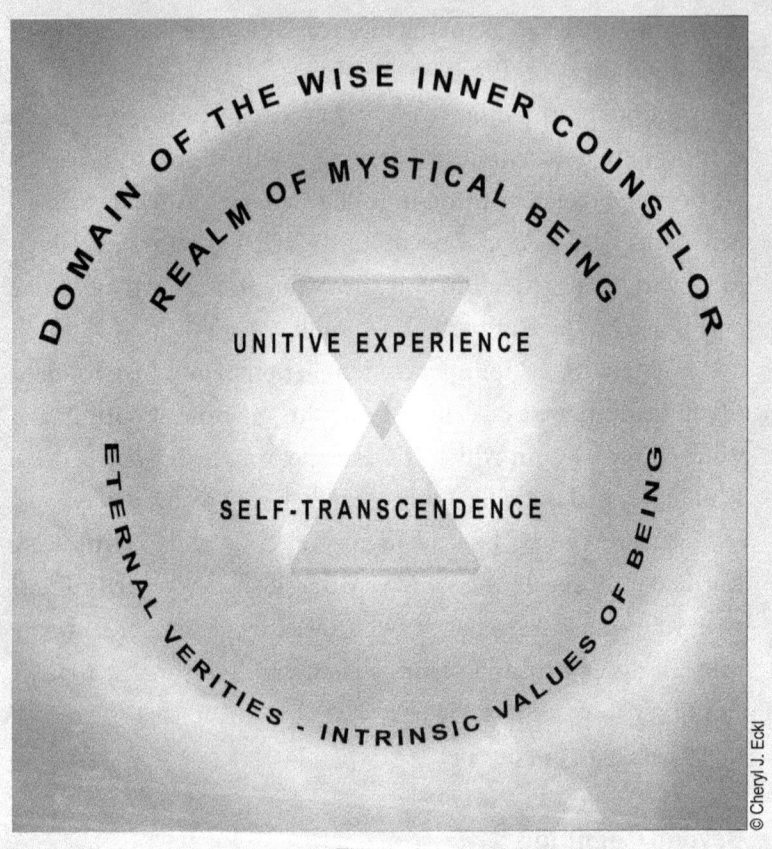

Figure 2

Showing a view of the relationship between
self-transcendence and the unitive experience.

———————

Metamotivated by the eternal verities (intrinsic values of Being),
a person who is pursuing a path of self-transcendence
may be absorbed into the unitive experience
where contact with the realm of mystical Being
becomes a way of living.

The entire process is enfolded within the domain
of The Wise Inner Counselor.

Chapter Fifteen

Entering Mystical Being

In a discussion with other psychologists that took place later in Maslow's life, he described how his own peak experiences had become less intense and less frequent. He considered this a good thing—perhaps Nature's way of protecting an aging body.

Instead, he found himself becoming "mythic, poetic, and symbolic about ordinary things."[33]

In this state of elevated consciousness, mystery, awe, and sacredness were present for him as in peak experiences. Only now they were constant, rather than occurring in a sudden burst of illumination.

Maslow said that the world looks this way "if the mystic experience really takes." In other words, if your peak experiences actually change your life, you can live in the miraculous and also function in the world in the manner of many great saints.

Teresa of Avila was such a person. She could experience profound mystical ecstasies and still run a monastery.

This is the goal of the Wise Inner Counselor—to guide our soul and outer awareness into perpetual communion with the sacred, so that the ordinary and the extraordinary dance together in the flow of everyday living.

Maslow called this state of equanimity "the plateau experience," which I think may give an unclear impression about the nature of the experience and what happens when we are in it.

Reconsidering the "Plateau"

Having spent a fair amount of time in the southwestern United States, when I hear the word "plateau," I think of a flat, static landscape or even a stagnant place of little activity.

The state of consciousness that Maslow was describing is neither static nor idle. While it does include sensations of peace and serene equipoise, it also is dynamic and filled with vital energy. Therefore, I would like to call this plane of Being the "unitive experience."

The unitive experience can be seen as the full flowering of Selfhood that produces the next turn of the spiral of Being. However, it is not a cognitive process. The human mind cannot figure out how to reach this state of being. My teacher explained that the unitive occurs because we transcend and transmute lesser levels of consciousness to such an extent that we and the Divine are actually absorbed into each other.

I know this mystical realm was very real to Maslow because he was immersed in it, integrating the many lessons he had learned, and assimilating the refined atmosphere of this higher state of Being. I get the sense that, for him, the unitive was becoming an end state that was joyful and deeply fulfilling.

Before his sudden heart attack in 1970, he had suffered a near-fatal episode in 1967. After that event, he began speaking to those close to him about being comfortable with the idea of dying. Still, he remained vibrant to the end of his life, even while exuding the peace and happiness of someone who has come to terms with his own mortality.

A Choice We Make

Maslow says that the unitive is more volitional than the sudden ignitions of insight and all-consuming revelations of peaks.

What this means to me is that we must be so in love with the Divine that lives within us and that is imminent in all of life that the greatest desire of our soul is to be subsumed into that presence. Therefore, much of our task on this journey to higher consciousness involves creating the circumstances in which the unitive experience can happen.

In other words, aspiring to the unitive is a choice we make. We do our inner work with the spiritual disciplines that even Maslow himself advocated. And then we let Love find a way to envelope us in the realm of mystical Being.

A Warning About Phenomena

Maslow developed a sober perspective on the longterm effects of living solely in the realm of mystical Being. He warned against complacency, or even laziness, that could occur in those who showed a tendency to become overly focused on achieving exalted states of consciousness.

This was rarely an issue for his psychologically healthy self-actualizers who were also balanced self-transcenders. The difficulty arose with those who had skipped the self-development phase of actualization and had jumped straight to phenomena as an escape from the complexities of daily life. The problem also could occur in self-transcenders who began pursuing phenomena as a way of overcoming metapathologies.

To Maslow, a sure sign of authentic self-transcendence was the person's ability to balance the demands of daily life with the lasting, positive effects of their peak experiences.

Sacralizing Deficiency-Needs

One of the remarkable characteristics of individuals who have achieved the unitive experience is their ability to see the sacred in the mundane. In this state, dichotomies have been resolved. Satisfied Deficiency-needs have been transmuted, elevated, and sacralized into expressions of refined awareness.

- Self-esteem is transformed into humility and honor for the divine spark within.
- The desire to belong has become the sense of belonging to the Divine, one in the cosmic ocean of Being.
- The soul is now safe in the heart's spiritual center where it has merged with the Wise Inner Counselor.
- The need for physical survival, while still of paramount importance to the continuation of our journey through life, is now pervaded by a vision of the soul's immortality.

The Luminous Unitive

We create our life according to what we can envision. There is a certain enchantment to living in the unitive realm of Being.

When we maintain the sunlit image of Self that transcends all lesser states of awareness, our perception can be filled with the eternal verities of the True, the Good, and the Beautiful. Those elements of consciousness will be reflected in the atmosphere we emanate and in the environment we fashion.

I am convinced that this vision is what Maslow attained at the end of his life. He projected his love for humanity out into the world in hopes that his ideas would catch fire and ignite that love in the psyche of millions, so they might perceive their own greatness and create the luminous life that he knew was possible.

Beyond Maslovian Psychology

Henry Geiger wrote that as Maslow aged, he became more philosophical. He found it was impossible "to isolate the pursuit of psychological truth from philosophical questions."[34]

Had Maslow lived longer, I wonder if he would have ceased being the philosophical scientist that Geiger described in favor of becoming fully a philosopher or even a poet?

The spherical spaciousness of the fully realized realm of mystical Being resists prose description. A world of nuance requires the indirect, the implicit, the suggested—in a word, the poetical that paints sublime word pictures to kindle the soul's attention and anchor meaning in the heart.

This is the razor's edge where being and doing unite in balanced synergy, complete and flowing with an elevated will in concert with the Divine.

Maroon Lake, Maroon Bells Wilderness Area
near Aspen, Colorado

Chapter Sixteen

Reflecting on Your Luminous Life - 2

When I first wrote a few website articles about Abraham Maslow and self-transcendence, I had no idea that my ongoing exploration of the person and the psychologist was going to take me to such depth and breadth.

Clearly, the inside of Maslow's mind and heart always held "more." And yet, my biggest take-away from reading hundreds of pages of his work is simple: He was a man who loved deeply and through his written and spoken words offered that love to as many people as he could possibly reach.

Your Thoughts?

I invite you to consider what has impressed you most about the popular professor who gave psychology a new language and who championed the right of every one of us to transcend any sense of limitation about the farthest reaches of our potential.

If we were together in person, I would set aside some time for each of us to tell a story about our best experience with love knowledge. We might describe the felt sense of that experience or how love knowledge relates to creating a luminous life.

I have a feeling that our storytelling time might need to take place during an evening meal. I can imagine a very rich conversation extending far into the night as our journey continues.

Part Three

Lighting a Candle in the Dark

Outwitting the Shadow Self

*The soul may be bruised
but is not scarred forever
when Love is realized
as its perpetual,
eternal essence.*

Chapter Seventeen

Digging Deep, Reaching High

I recently received a newsletter from an associate who is a management consultant. He said that depths within each person remain more unknown than known. I agree, which raises the question: How do we bring the unknown to the surface? Often the answer lies in dealing with interferences that reveal our hidden strengths and weaknesses.

Obstacles Provide the Means
Without obstacles we probably would not be challenged to dig deep into often-untapped inner resources. Without challenges to our current circumstances, we would have little reason to reach for higher consciousness.

We study our psychology in order to transcend it. To become better than our foibles. To assimilate the wisdom, love, and fortitude of our Wise Inner Counselor. To embody the sacred to which our soul aspires. To make a positive difference to our fellow travelers on this journey through life.

We do not fear roadblocks to self-transcendence.

We welcome opportunities to sharpen our perception of what is real and what is unreal. We strive to meet these difficulties with gratitude, with the solid rock of the Being-values of the True Self. This is how we light a candle that swallows up the darkness of the egoic, shadow self.

Dichotomies at the Core

Dr. Maslow was very clear about how concrete divisions can create serious obstacles to reaching our potential. He said that dichotomies can cause pathologies. And pathologies often are the root of dichotomies. Isolating two parts of a whole that need each other distorts and weakens them both.[35]

Here is a succinct definition of how the false self operates to create separations that render two vital elements of anyone or anything mutually exclusive. This split is especially devastating when the soul is separated from the True Self by past experiences or current responses to life's circumstances.

I must ask myself: Does my response to any situation separate me from my Wise Inner Counselor? If I have fallen into a negative pattern of thought, feeling, or action, how can I reverse that momentum to one of compassion and unity? How can I elevate my consciousness to the realm of Being-cognition?

Confronting the Anti-Hero

Living a life of self-transcendence truly is a hero's journey. Sometimes I feel like the mythological Greek hero Theseus who ventured into the labyrinth to slay the Minotaur, a creature that was devouring Athenian youth.

The imagery is vivid and the metaphor is not far off when dealing with an old psychological pattern that may arise from the subconscious like an anti-hero, often at very inopportune times.

This is the shadow self—the counterfeit identity that usurps the authority and presence of the authentic Self. It lurks, skulks, anticipates my best efforts, and seems intent on sabotaging those endeavors with doubt, fear, and mental confusion.

It is shocking to realize that any of us could be harboring such an unreal identity. This does not make us terrible people.

However, it does mean that we must dig deep into resolving our unhealthy patterns of thought, feeling, and behavior in order to liberate our soul from the false self that threatens to consume it.

Spiritual Bypass

A challenge for some psychologically immature individuals is a desire to escape into meditation or phenomena generated by peak experiences. This is spiritual bypass.

We actually achieve the mystical through the practical, which means dealing with our psychology and transmuting the egoic self. Otherwise, we may be creating a light-filled patina that gives us the appearance of saintliness until something triggers an outburst of anger that turns the aura inside out.

I once experienced this with a woman who wanted to buy a house I owned. She eagerly shared her mystical experiences and presented herself as a spiritually advanced person.

However, when a requirement for the sale arose that she did not like, she became angry and abusive. The bypass she had erected on her spiritual path broke down over what was a minor challenge that we could have resolved.

Stagnation and Non-Resolution

Unresolved grief or other emotions can block the flow of the regenerating energy that supports self-transcendence. If we do not develop a felt sense of being revitalized by our life (even when we are completely spent), we likely are not transcending. We may be running very fast in one spot, or we may have stopped moving altogether.

Stagnation is a treacherous place to be.

Not long ago I failed an important test that left me feeling really defeated. In situations like, that I try to follow the emotions back to their source, knowing that some kind of fear is usually at the bottom of my reaction. I eventually discovered a huge pocket of unresolved grief over the death of my teacher. She had died exactly one year to the day after Stephen's passing, so my grief over losing him had taken precedence.

I have done a lot of inner work on the loss of my husband, but I had never fully grieved my teacher's death. Instead, those feelings had gone underground into my subconscious where they stayed until a seemingly unrelated event triggered an exaggerated emotional response that I was finally able to process.

Summoning the Presence of Love

The fact that I had to wrestle with the strong emotions of this situation illustrates to me that the journey of self-transcendence is a very complete one. Old sorrows or hurts or traumas do not go away simply because we do not remember them.

Although such records of the past are largely unseen, they are present in subtle ways that are part of the fearful self and its defense mechanisms that we may fail to notice until they erupt.

It is not easy to welcome those eruptions that are painful, even shameful. Still, I know from experience that when we can summon the indwelling presence of Love, we find the strength to face and transmute emotions linked to situations that our soul could not handle earlier in this or another lifetime.

Resistance to One's Mission

Sometimes even the ablest people will balk when confronted with a part or the whole of their mission that they do not want to face. Maslow called this tendency the "Jonah Complex," named after the Old Testament prophet who tried to shirk his duty until he spent three illuminating days in the belly of a whale.

Still, Maslow was convinced that humans need challenges to quicken inner growth. He perceived value in life's inevitable difficulties, as did his self-transcenders who seemed to take reverses of fortune in stride.

These people liked to exercise their problem-solving ability and they seldom became complacent. They would purposefully seek out ways to continue striving. If they discerned resistance bubbling up in their consciousness, they looked for reasons in their psychology and eliminated the cause as soon as possible.

When Self-Actualization Is a Barrier

Too much of a good thing can turn into a detriment if we forget who is the real doer of our endeavors. In striving to fulfill our potential, the temptation to start taking our accomplishments for granted can lead to self-aggrandizement instead of actualization.

I have always admired Maslow's description of people who love their profession and cannot imagine doing anything else. There is a sense of humility about the career they view as a sacred labor. They seem to function in a state of perpetual gratitude for the life they are allowed to live while doing this work.

I remember my father-in-law exclaiming how much he enjoyed his job and how grateful he was to be paid well for doing what he loved. Such delight in one's life work makes me think that gratitude and humility are "Being-attitudes" that are vital to creating a luminous life.

Chapter Eighteen

No Sympathy for the Shadow

One of the standard tactics of the imposter is to whisper in our ear, tempting us into sympathy for its supposed plight. I call this "shadow-sympathy" because it hides in the dark places of consciousness. It agrees with the counterfeit self and follows it into the ditch of discouragement, depression, and despair.

Shadow-sympathy is the inversion of compassion. In the guise of human niceness, the shadow casts over our soul a sticky-sweet pall of mediocrity that limits our determination to unite with our Wise Inner Counselor.

In our hearts we know we've got divinity in us. But the shadow's "poor sweet baby" refrain can drown out the voice of Love that urges us to stand tall, plug into that extra gear we all possess, and beat the odds of foreboding prophecy.

Life is challenging enough without voices of doom who spout the dogma of conformity that tries to homogenize our mind into gray nothingness. This is the not-self that shows up in fine apparel designed to hide its shallowness as it appropriates our soul's innate love for the deep mysteries of Being.

Challenges of Shadow-Sympathy
Shadow-sympathy gets us into a lot of messes—complex tangles of negative emotion, a sense of injustice, the desire to get even with persons or situations, many of them long past.

The shadow whines for our attention. It builds alliances out of prejudice, bias, misunderstanding, and sometimes from half-truths or intentional fabrications. Like a slow Internet connection, it interferes with clear hearing and seeing by reducing the bandwidth of perception to a myopic peephole.

Shadow-sympathy reinforces narrow opinions and blocks the other side of the story. It may lead well-meaning people into superficial views that work at cross-purposes to their espoused values. It promotes a sense of victimhood that does disservice to the soul it claims to help.

Notoriously gossipy, this usurper deters discernment and drags self-awareness down to levels that discourage soul growth. It ensnares the unwitting because it rests on the shifting sands of fads and fancies. It cannot stand on an inner truth that it does not contain.

The shadow preys upon the faint of heart and keeps them weak and feeble-minded. It saps the inner fire needed to take bold action. It is tepid and sometimes testy when confronted with the energetic demands of the greater Love that compassion calls us to express toward all of life.

The False Sacrifice

I have observed a serious consequence of being embroiled in shadow-sympathy as what my teacher called "the false sacrifice." Here an individual gives and gives—not from the inexhaustible fount of Love that is the essence of inner wisdom, but rather from the very fabric of their soul.

In this situation the giver who does not regularly dip into the reservoirs of Love from which all noble action is derived becomes exhausted and resentful.

However, when we know we are acting as an instrument of inner-directed care, we are not depleted. The more we allow our

True Self to act, the greater is the compassion we have available to offer to life.

Compassion champions the best in all of us. It is the determination we share to accelerate our consciousness. Built upon our honor for the divine spark in the heart of our Self and others, it aims for the stars and scales the heights of possibility.

Compassion is mutually enhancing. When we support another person's wholeness, we are acting in consonance with their Wise Inner Counselor and our own.

Shadow-sympathy is mutually depleting. Just because we experience energy moving between us and another person does not mean it is rising. We may feel temporary elation, even a sense of well-being. But what is the lasting consequence?

What effect did our interaction have in the long run? Did we encourage the soul or appease the shadow? What are the fruits of our actions? By those fruits we may discern if we were being truly compassionate or merely sympathetic.

Avoiding the Swamp of Shadow-Sympathy

Compassion offers practical assistance so our fellow travelers may raise themselves up out of their troubles. It places the onus for transformation on the individual who is burdened, not on the one who desires to lighten the weight of their cares.

One of the best ways to help someone take responsibility for their difficulties is to engage them in creative problem-solving, which can activate their own inner wisdom that will supply a solution. This way the one who is suffering may gain a sense of hope, courage, and the victory of their own accomplishment.

When we kindle the light of spiritual fire in ourselves and our companions, shadow-sympathy fades away into the swamp of its own inadequacy.

Holding Tight to Inner Guidance

Outwitting the shadow is a bit like playing the old game of Whack-a-Mole. The creature raises its head and is immediately revealed. We see it and smack it down with spiritual practice, psychological awareness, and practical action. Then it pops up again somewhere else, perhaps more subtly this time, hoping we won't notice.

The farther we ascend the spiral of Being, the sneakier the shadow becomes. Our job is to remember that fact and bank a reservoir of light energy in our being so the darkness will register on our internal radar.

We may find ourselves approaching a ditch or slippery slope of circumstance, but we do not have to fall in or slide backward. Instead, we hold tight to our Wise Inner Counselor whose guidance is the surety that we will survive to create more transcendent tomorrows while encouraging others to do the same.

Overcoming Shadow-Irritation

I have identified a flip side of sympathy in my own consciousness as irritation or frustration that life isn't moving along the way I want it to. I recently read that when events are not unfolding at the speed I think they should, the Universe probably is operating on a different timetable.

In such cases I have realized a need for what could be called "patient daring"—the courage to resist immediate action. And to relax into the divine will that can make itself known when the time is right.

When I put my Wise Inner Counselor back in the driver's seat of my life, I find myself surmounting obstacles with amazing ease—probably because I had erected many of those barriers in the first place.

My being strong-willed can be useful when decisive action is required. However, human willfulness is not useful when my desires have set up dichotomies that block the flow.

Service Can Outwit the Shadow

Regardless of an obstacle's source, lighting a candle of Selfhood in service to others is often an answer.

In fact, George W. Russell (Æ) wrote that there are fewer hindrances in life than we might think. He says that wherever there is a soul in need, there is likely another soul willing to help.

Throughout the many dramas in our lifetime we will play both parts. The difference lies in how we fill those roles so that the service we offer comes from the heart, not the ego.

What Kind of Service?

A friend and I were discussing how little the concept of service is really understood because the word is used in different contexts. We were pondering what it actually means to serve selflessly.

Maslow is helpful here. He uses the word "unselfconscious" to describe service that is non-manipulative. What he means is that psychologically healthy people are able to spontaneously respond to someone else's need without referencing themselves.

Conversely, the egoic self is very conscious of how its actions are playing to the world it considers its audience.

I once watched a sitcom program on television in which the main character was patting himself on the back for doing a good deed. "I am such a good person," he said with a smug expression of self-satisfaction.

That is Deficiency-service aimed at filling in a lack in the giver's consciousness.

Avoiding Burnout

Offering service also brings up the concept of self-care. When I was conducting workshops for The Denver Hospice, I spoke to a group of home healthcare nurses on the subject of burnout.

These were inspiring people who faced heart-wrenching situations in the homes of many who were desperate for help. Because the needs were so great, these nurses often found it difficult to keep going, even though this was their chosen profession.

When I asked about their experience of burnout, one senior nurse said, "My give-a-damn light goes out."

What a great expression for an obstacle to service faced by those who are dedicated to giving it. I could tell that most of these nurses were acting from a profound calling to work in a challenging industry. Yet they needed a way to prevent themselves from exceeding their physical, mental, and emotional capacity to serve.

Inner Guidance Is the Key

As family caregivers we often must serve our loved ones beyond what we think we can give. When I faced those moments, I quickly learned that the key to staying afloat was attunement with my Wise Inner Counselor. With that connection in place, I found that any Deficiency-needs that arose in me were less likely to derail me when my loved one needed me the most.

I also have found that letting someone know my prayers are with them as they face a major hurdle may be the best care I can offer. My inner guide knows when I should be physically present or when my spiritual service is perhaps even more effective.

Chapter Nineteen

The Danger of Collectives

The false self is sneaky. It is a master of disguise. Whoever first wrote about a magical cloaking device or an invisibility cape surely had confronted the shadow's ability to hide in the fabric of our consciousness. We are so accustomed to its presence, we take no notice until it does something truly egregious.

Collectives act in the same way. We and they are so intricately woven together that we do not notice the subtle ways in which groups we belong to may be attempting to control us.

No matter how well-meaning, human associations can be a poor substitute for communion with our inner divinity. Remembering that fact can strengthen our resolve to honor the spark of illumination that originally prompted us to fulfill our potential.

Outer Collectives

Families are collectives. So are organizations, professional clubs, and gangs. One thing they have in common is their desire to retain their members. When individuals decide to leave, their potential departure threatens the survival of the entire group.

Because of this reaction, transcenders often face opposition from those closest to them. These folks may bemoan what they view as abandonment by their friend or loved one who is simply trying to live the life that he or she was born for.

"Stick to your guns" is my best advice in these situations. The transition may be difficult, but not following your heart and the guidance of your Wise Inner Counselor can be much worse. These confrontations can be painful reminders that creating genuine Self-esteem is an inside job.

Inner Collectives

These are the tricky ones because they operate primarily in the subconscious. We may catch sight of them only in retrospect.

I like to imagine these inner groups as if they were a cast of characters—perhaps leftovers from past lives. We all have been princes and paupers, chancellors and chambermaids.

As part of a psychology course, I once wrote a skit with twelve characters who came to life in my imagination as aspects of my psychology. Some were positive, others were not. None of them was really evil, but there were a few who vigorously opposed the positive characters. This was a humorous and very effective method for revealing how some elements of my false self were opposing my True Self.

Actors often relish portraying the bad guys. That is a very good way to objectify certain undesirable traits of the human psyche that are best left to storytelling. Acting the part of a villain is highly preferable to your subconscious "acting out."

In real life the time to invoke light into an unhealthy pattern and transmute it is when it appears. Sometimes we have very little time in which to do so.

With What Do We Identify?

I would like to share a story from the life of a brilliant man who had a revelation following the tragic death of the young woman who was the love of his life. He had not been present when she died, so he wrote her a letter in his diary describing how her death had shown him the uselessness of his ego.

He had been a very self-absorbed person. However, his beloved's intensely joyful spirituality and courageous acceptance of her terminal illness had demonstrated to him how a soul can be elevated. That experience changed him. In his letter he wrote that he now understood the oneness of Spirit in life and in death. He seemed to draw great solace from this realization.

Unfortunately, it did not last.

Only weeks later, he went through a terrifying episode that Maslow would have called a "desolation experience" (the opposite of an uplifting peak experience). The man seems to have caught a glimpse of his false self as a severely damaged figure. His description reminded me of Gollum from *The Hobbit*.

Instead of realizing that this was part of an inner collective rising up to drag him back to self-absorption, the man decided that the figure was his actual self. In fact, he declared, "I am that." He immediately fell into a debilitating depression that lasted for months. He had seen the light, but could not hold it.

My Own Experience

Fortunately, the event I am going to share with you was not anything like a psychotic break. However, it was illustrative of how protective the shadow is of its inner collective.

The Sunday in question was a see-saw kind of day. After a severe morning snowstorm and computer problems that had nearly destroyed months of work on this book, in the afternoon I had a spiritual epiphany that lasted for several hours.

Later that evening I was prompted to breathe a prayer for help with my meditation practice. Instantly I started choking and coughing—an obvious reaction from an inner collective that was up to no good.

I soon calmed the coughing fit and said another prayer

to reconnect with my True Self. I also did some inner spiritual work to dissolve the unhealthy psychology that had so suddenly opposed a delicate inner communion.

I was grateful to be reminded that the shadow can be triggered simply by our connection with the Divine. Our safety lies in remembering who we really are and in identifying with the divine spark in our heart so we are not thrown off course by the imposter's masquerades or dramas.

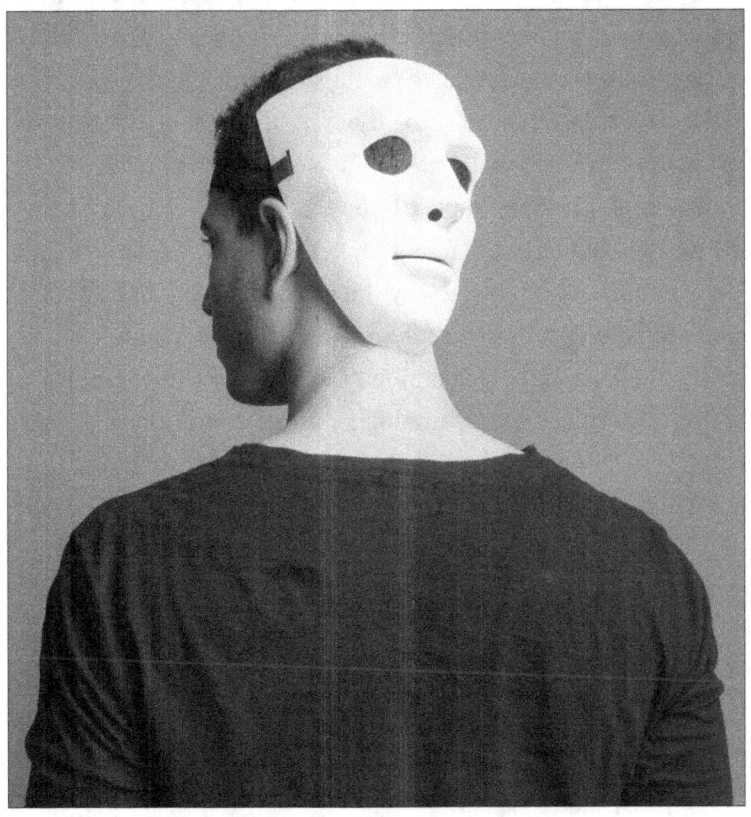

Chapter Twenty

Metapathologies - Cause or Effect?

As I mentioned earlier, Maslow observed that once we have tasted of the Being-realm's sublime atmosphere, any subsequent thwarting of our higher-order needs can result in the psychological response he called "metapathologies."

These conditions can be thought of as a soul sickness that is different from mental illness. When observed from the outside, metapathologies may appear to be the source of blocks to transcendence, but they are not. They are symptoms—the effects of denying our ability to embody the values of Being that function like needs. When those needs are not satisfied, we suffer.

Blocks to our communion with our Wise Inner Counselor may also result in metapathologies. These conditions can make us feel as if we were all alone in an alien universe, dying of thirst for a different kind of water than what everyone else is drinking.

Here is a short list of metapathologies taken from Maslow's extensive observations:

- Apathy
- Boredom
- Cynicism
- Despair - discontent - disillusionment
- Frustrated idealism
- Hopelessness
- Loss of zest for life
- Nihilism

- Sense of powerlessness
- Wondering why you cannot seem to find the kindred souls who are your fellow travelers in life

Knowledge Can Liberate

Sometimes just learning about the existence of metapathologies can make all the difference in how we perceive ourselves. This phenomenon revealed itself when I conducted an introductory workshop on Maslow's theory of human needs.

When I shared some of his most commonly observed characteristics of self-transcenders, a young woman in the audience became very excited. When I showed a flip chart containing the short list of metapathologies, she lit up like a sunrise.

Here was the answer she had been seeking to many of the difficult emotions she had dealt with since childhood. She had always felt very different from her classmates. She could see life more clearly than others, and she knew there was more to living on planet Earth than what her peers were interested in exploring.

Now she knew why her friends often did not understand her. Hers was the language of Being spoken by poets, mystics, and seers. And she was highly motivated by the intrinsic values.

When this young woman identified herself as a natural self-transcender, her life changed.

From Darkness to Light

I highly value the service that my colleagues in the mental health arena provide for healing those who are truly burdened. Counseling from a transpersonal psychologist definitely helped me during several periods of extreme emotional distress.

Sometimes the perspective of a counselor, mentor, life coach, or friend who has seen it all can alleviate the anxiety of feeling as if you were the only person in the world dealing with your issues.

One reason Maslow developed transpersonal psychology is that self-transcenders who are in the midst of metapathologies require the understanding of a therapist who is familiar with the intrinsic mysticism and metaneeds of Being-cognition. This approach is quite different from traditional psychoanalysis or other modalities.

A serious complication can arise when clinicians who are not attuned to the delicacy of the transcendent soul perceive metapathologies as mental illness, which they routinely medicate. They also may inadvertently dredge up memories of trauma from this or past lifetimes that the person is not psychologically strong enough to face.

I was fortunate in my choice of counselor. Finding a good match for your situation may require some research.

Encouraging Flow

I see the stultifying *ennui* of metapathologies as similar to many manifestations of grief. Both experiences can stop the flow of energy that maintains vitality of body, mind, and soul and that can revive the enervated sense of Self.

Over the years I have discovered some helpful activities for priming the pump of life-giving energy that nurtures resilience. And yet, writing this chapter has prompted me to look further into the essence of the benefit.

A Meditation on Beauty's Helpfulness

When I contemplate the effects of sitting by moving water or walking in Nature or going to a museum, the quality at the core of these activities is the presence of heart-opening beauty.

The connection with beauty elevates my soul past obstacles or the perception of obstacles, which often is the same. As others have done before me, I change my perception by turning my outward eye to the beauty of form in art and unspoiled landscape.

Wordsworth and his sister, Dorothy, often walked eight miles over Lake District pathways to post a letter. Having wandered those paths myself, I see how the landscape's beauty would have elevated their minds and hearts above daily challenges.

For relief from his own burdens, Emerson depended upon the lush Concord, Massachusetts, countryside where the serenity of Walden Pond lay but a short walk from his doorstep.

The beauty of classical music would send Maslow into ecstasies, and Æ found solace from Dublin's urban greyness in the green, green fields and Atlantic vistas of Éire.

"What about the soul beauty of people?" my Wise Inner Counselor asks. The answer is easy.

When I am out and about these days, I experience a sort of inner radar that picks up on an element of beauty in a person. I may notice their eyes or hair or a piece of clothing that reflects their inner beauty, which I can feel when I comment on their outer beauty. They smile and thank me for the compliment—which is a completion. In an instant of connection, two souls are raised above the mundanity of the marketplace.

"Now consider the inner landscape," says the voice of Love.

Ah, yes! The elevated thought I may find in the gorgeous words of masterful writers, or in my own meditations upon the divine presence within, propels me into a unitive experience where there are no barriers. Only the formless beauty of elegant, exquisite, ineffable light. Truly, the key to beauty's helpfulness is revealed in connection.

A golden September afternoon at the Maroon Bells Wilderness Area near Aspen, Colorado

Chapter Twenty-One

One of the Biggest Obstacles

To my mind, a very serious impediment to self-transcendence is ignorance—either our own or the willful withholding from us of vital information we need for our own soul growth.

For starters, we have been left in the dark about our true nature. Divinity is alive in us as the Wise Inner Counselor. But that basic tenet of perennial wisdom has been hidden from many of us by our faith or cultural traditions.

Equally limiting to our enlightenment, some thought systems have denied the universal law of cause and effect known as karma. They also have dismissed karma's sibling concept of past lives, which is known around the world as reincarnation.[36]

We Have Lived Before

One of the welcome surprises from my research for this book was that renowned poets and philosophers from the late eighteenth and early nineteenth centuries were familiar with ancient texts that spoke openly about reincarnation and karma.

Even John Adams commented on this wisdom literature in his correspondence with fellow ex-president Thomas Jefferson.[37]

The book that stood out for many was the *Bhagavad-Gita*. One of my favorite passages from the *Gita* offers a beautifully succinct explanation of reincarnation in an often-repeated verse from the 1885 translation by Sir Edwin Arnold:

> Never the spirit was born;
> The spirit shall cease to be never;
> Never was time it was not;
> End and Beginning are dreams!
> Birthless and deathless and changeless
> Remaineth the spirit for ever;
> Death has not touched it at all,
> Dead though the house of it seems!

England's Poet Laureate Understood

William Wordsworth was also familiar with literature of the East. The following lines from *Ode: Intimations of Immortality* provide a clear example of his awareness of past lives.

> Our birth is but a sleep and a forgetting:
> The Soul that rises with us, our life's Star,
> Hath had elsewhere its setting,
> And cometh from afar:
> Not in entire forgetfulness,
> And not in utter nakedness,
> But trailing clouds of glory do we come
> From God, who is our home:[38]

Means and Ends

In multiple lifetimes we have made positive and negative karma. Simply stated, karma is the law that "what goes around comes around." We reap what we have sown.

We are subject to the effects of causes we have set in motion—a thousand years ago or only this morning in rush-hour traffic. The law operates impersonally, which Emerson seems to have comprehended early in life.

At the beginning of his essay titled *Compensation* he states that he had wanted to compose such a discourse since he was a boy. As an adult he wrote:

> Every act rewards itself, or, in other words, integrates itself....Crime and punishment grow out of one stem.... Cause and effect, means and ends, seed and fruit, cannot be severed; the effect already blooms in the cause, the end preëxists in the means, the fruit in the seed.[39]

Whether we realize it or not, portions of the shadow self that manifest as fears, unhealthy behaviors, difficult relationships, illnesses of mind or body may have originated in prior ages. References to that understanding in spiritual texts of East and West remain veiled from many populations.

Seeking a Remedy

What are we to do, then, if we have been rendered ignorant of how ancient and varied our debts to life may be? These are barriers to our psychological health that counseling or therapy alone cannot fix. Knowledge of spiritual realities is required.

Each of us is a tapestry woven of myriad threads that represent thousands of lifetimes lived for good and for ill. Our task is to pull out the dingy, outworn threads so the golden ones may shine through.

We are fortunate that in this age there is a method for untangling life's knottiest problems. For the first time in several millennia, we have access to a technique that was previously available only to advanced spiritual adepts—an energy that can work miracles.

Chapter Twenty-Two

The Miracle of Invoking Light

I am in love with sound. I always have been. For years I made my living with sound—as a singer, actor, instructor, and speaker. Long before I took up my pen as a writer, sound and I were constant companions.

That love affair assumed a more profound meaning when I learned about the power of mantras and chants that actually invoke spiritual light into the material plane. How incredible to realize we can change circumstances for the better with sound!

I know that this daily practice has sustained my spiritual journey. In fact, I am certain it has saved my life more than once.

At the End of My Rope

I graduated from college with a degree in theater arts and absolutely no plan for the future. Other than wanting to be an actor and singer, my thoughts about a career were vague at best. I drifted between mindless jobs and fruitless auditions and fell in with a crowd of basically good people who, nevertheless, were part of the sex, drugs, and rock-n-roll culture.

I remember telling a friend that I felt like a pawn of the Universe, buffeted hither and thither by the prevailing winds of circumstance.

One day I had a vision of my guardian angel looking like a soldier limping home from the Civil War with a head wound, arm in a sling, and leaning on a single crutch. I realized then that

I had reached the end of my rope. This was one of those pivotal times in my life when I surrendered my human will. I knew I needed help and I asked for it.

Fortunately, the Divine is never as far away as we might think. I happened to visit some former theater friends who had been part of a spiritual community. When we went out to eat after the show they were performing in, I was able to share my plight with them.

They eagerly told me that, in the face of the most difficult situations, I could invoke light from a position of partnership with Spirit and give that light back to the Divine to resolve the problems that were beyond me.

This was a revolutionary concept. And it was only the beginning of what turned out to be an all-night conversation that changed my life.

Affirming the Sacredness of Being

My friends explained that what was once a strictly religious teaching is now so mainstream as to perhaps require no specific mention—except to say that acknowledging the innate sacredness of our innermost nature is one of the surest ways to accelerate our ascent into the consciousness of illumined Being.

When we say, "I AM," we are affirming the presence of the Divine in us. When we find ourselves in a muddle of internal or external obstacles, saying "I AM Light!" is one of the most useful affirmations we can give.

The Miracle Energy

They also explained that, despite the revelations of spiritual teachers, adepts, and psychologists, we cannot merely think, talk, or meditate our way out of our troubles.

We need a method that "un-creates" patterns of negativity, pain, and a thousand misdeeds from this and other lifetimes of which we may not be consciously aware. That really caught my attention, especially when they told me that in the early twentieth century a powerful tool for transmutation had been released to humanity. This is the miracle energy of the violet light which people throughout the ages have seen as spiritual fire.

This was not a difficult visualization for me. When I was a child, I would spend hours sitting in front of my family's fireplace meditating on the flames. One year my father brought home some special logs that made a rainbow of colors as they burned. I had always been partial to the golden-yellow ones. After my friends' revelations, I soon became a fan of the violet.

Invoking this spiritual fire became my go-to practice because I could feel it accelerating my consciousness. Sometimes I would see a glimmering of violet in my mind's eye. Most often I would feel its energy swirling around me and warming my heart.

I am still amazed that sound can change energy. Yet, after giving mantras to invoke the violet flame, I always feel lighter—as if density, toxicity, negative thoughts and feelings, or records of past actions have been transmuted into pure, radiant light.

Over the years I have noticed this miracle flame nurturing a deeper contact with my Wise Inner Counselor that has dramatically improved my intuition.

Mercy and Forgiveness

I am convinced that the violet fire can act as a healing balm of mercy and forgiveness to ourselves and others—even to the world when we visualize its highly vibrating energy pouring into dire situations around the globe.

I know this radiant light has eased many burdens in my

life. On one poignant occasion I experienced deep resolution between myself and a friend from whom I had become estranged.

Other friends and I have discussed how using the violet flame has helped us forgive each other for misunderstandings that could have driven a wedge between us.

We have forgiven life for disappointing us. We have forgiven the Divine for not preventing the lawful return of our karma so we could transmute it. And we have managed to forgive ourselves for the times we have gone off course on our spiritual journey.

Life Can Be Vibrant

The false self is unrelentingly crafty. Many times I have failed to anticipate its subterfuge. Yet I know in my heart that as long as I am accelerating the communion between my soul and inner guidance by invoking the violet light, I may not be required to learn every scenario in the shadow's playbook.

I now understand that what the journey of self-transcendence *does* require from each of us is that we continue to transmute the psychological vulnerabilities that keep us blind to the betrayer in our midst. When our soul sees through that darkness, we are no longer deceived.

The violet flame can clear our vision and free us to be so bonded to our authentic Self that the consciousness of error is finally starved out of existence because we have stopped feeding it. When we nurture the truth of our being with light, life can be more vibrant with every passing day.

The Remedy Is Within Reach

There have been times when my unreal self (or that of someone else) has tried to beat me up because of my human imperfections.

Projections like this can be hard to overcome. Still, I know that no matter what deterrents I may face, the remedy is within reach.

Invoking the miraculous energy of transmutation into those situations makes all the difference. The luminous life I am blessed to live today is proof. The violet flame really does work![40]

One More Thing

As I am writing this, I am seeing in my mind's eye a vivid image of my guardian angel, who is stronger than ever.

Healing the wounds my protector sustained on my behalf took a while, but angels are very resilient—especially when the person they watch over is taking responsibility for invoking the miracle light of transmutation.

I thought you would like to know.

Chapter Twenty-Three

Reflecting on Your Luminous Life - 3

You may be familiar with creating a fire ceremony as a ritual for transmutation. I would like to tell you a story about such an event that I conducted during a weekend retreat on transforming grief into power, meaning, and peace.

This ritual was deeply meaningful to the participants and to me, because we gave ourselves permission to retain positive personal attributes or circumstances that were still important, while we discarded worn-out elements of consciousness. Perhaps this story will inspire you to create a similar activity.

The Gathering

Eight spiritually oriented women joined me at a spacious retreat center located on the high grasslands and pinion pine forests of northern New Mexico. The surrounding landscape offered wide vistas that invited our inner and outer vision to expand into numinous planes of consciousness.

Many of the women (myself included) were inspired to write poetry and personal reflections about our experiences. The sharing was rich with poignant insights that helped everyone gain new appreciation for the portal into realms of beingness the grief journey can provide.

A Healing Process

I have noticed that discussions of loss often focus on letting go, which can actually be wounding to a newly grieving person. For many years now, my perspective has been that elements of our psychology and circumstances have a way of letting go of us when they are complete.

In the meantime I have observed how cherishing the memories, belongings, and stories that still have meaning for us can allow us to gradually integrate the essence of who or what we have lost. As the treasures we retain for a while naturally let go of us, our hearts can grow stronger and more wise.

The Ceremony

Although the weekend event was held during a very warm August, on Saturday evening we built a roaring fire in the adobe and stone fireplace that anchored the heart of the retreat center, which originally had been built as a private home.

Earlier in the day I had given each woman two envelopes. One was labeled RETAIN and the other RELEASE. During personal reflection time in the afternoon, we each wrote on slips of paper whatever issues we were prompted to place in our envelopes.

After dinner we gave mantras and chants to create a sacred space. When everyone felt ready, we took turns placing a paper from the RELEASE envelope into the flames until each woman was content that she had let go of whatever she needed to discard.

Some of the deepest sharing arose when we began spontaneously speaking aloud what we were retaining and what we were releasing. It was a very nurturing and healing experience.

After safely dousing the flames in the fireplace, we took our leave in silence that night and concluded the retreat on Sunday with a meditative walk around the retreat's outdoor labyrinth.

None of us was the same after that.

Fire Ceremony

Meet me at the hearth, said the noble guide,
and I will show you how to rest in Light,
while I illumine your ancient fear
of mystic dreams you've sought to escape,
though fleeing has not served you well.

Sit with me by the warmth of flame,
and welcome mysteries
that call you forth.

You have the power at your fingertips,
joy's wisdom folded in your cloak.

The underground seed is set to bloom,
and many old ways are letting go.
Allow what is false to slip away,
and be transition's fresh offspring.

A cleansing fire burns brightly now.
Be ready, dear soul, for transformation.
The Light in you is rising at last.

Part Four

Creativeness is Transcending

Bringing Your Light to Life

Viewed from Spirit's vantage seat
the way stays open for willing hearts
who love much what they do not see
and cherish those whose touch
they know as real.

Chapter Twenty-Four

MUSING ON THE MYSTERY

Creativeness is the song my soul sings. It is a mystery that leads me into undiscovered inner landscapes. Along the way I have come to know creativeness as a spiritual force, an innate facet of my soul, a source of unspeakable joy, and a portal for rich communion with my Wise Inner Counselor.

These days I find the spirit of creativeness urging me into deeper meditation on its meaning and joyful musings on future possibilities just waiting to be explored.

Your Soul Fragrance

Creativeness percolates through the beautiful image in which you are made. Your expression of that image exudes a soul fragrance that is uniquely yours and different from every other individual in the universe. Your soul fragrance imbues all that you create, from the smallest idea or gesture to the fullness of the luminous life you are actualizing.

When I taught a management course on critical thinking and creative problem solving, I discovered that students tended to believe that they either were or were not creative. I loved teaching this course because of how quickly it eliminated those stereotypical opinions.

Thinking back on how the light of illumination was ignited in many of the so-called "non-creatives," I see now that they were not only learning techniques for stimulating new ideas. They also were getting acquainted with their own soul fragrance.

That was an exciting development to witness. I often felt like a midwife attending the birth of the students' realization that they possessed an inborn capacity to create a life rich with meaning, both personally and professionally.

Your Glimmering Sense of Purpose

Every soul is born with a mission and a fervent desire to fulfill it. That is why you are here on planet Earth. To many, this *raison d'être* is the sacred labor—your glimmering sense of purpose.[41]

Creativeness includes the blueprint, the internal resources, the love, and the inspiration necessary to bring into the physical plane the gifts that only you can offer to a world in need.

Expressing your creativeness is where the partnership between your soul, your outer awareness, and your Wise Inner Counselor goes beyond self-actualization to ignite those moments of transcendent inspiration—the experiences that can lift you into the realm of mystical Being.

Creativeness and transcendence fit together. The terms are interchangeable. Engaging creativeness leads to transcendence, which inspires new ways of expressing creativeness. Each enhances the other like intertwining ribbons of light.

Maintaining the Conversation

As innovative beings we are constantly in motion, expanding in every direction with every new star in the universe. We grow and our achievements grow with us.

While we are evolving, we strive to maintain an ongoing conversation between our soul and our inner guide. Creativeness provides the energy and the context for that communion. This is where life sparkles, where we transcend the mundane, where the veil lifts between this world and the next, where we discover who and what we were always meant to be.

Building a Wisdom Boat

My Wise Inner Counselor reminds me that transcending the earth-bound self is like building a boat of refined awareness that will carry my soul from one enlightening shore to the next.

In a way, creativeness is that boat. The capacity to create can be like a vessel filled with treasures of wisdom, love, strength, and talent beyond our imagining. Our innate creativeness becomes a vehicle used in tandem by the soul and the Wise Inner Counselor to transport us from here to there.

As we let go of habits and behaviors that only serve to block the development of our glimmering sense of purpose, we add capacity to our wisdom boat, closing the gap between this world of form and the invisible world of Spirit.

When we pay focused attention to inner promptings, the depths of our appreciation increase for the unfailing presence of Love that lives within us. We find ourselves placing greater trust in our Wise Inner Counselor[42] who reciprocates by placing greater trust in us as creative partners.

Embracing the Twilight

It is natural to think of transcending the shadow self as stepping into the bright, active light of day that dispels the darkness that hangs onto us. Yet there are times when the twilight atmosphere of mystery calls.

My teacher often spoke of displacing the shadow with light and then replacing it with a more illumined perception of a value we are meant to espouse. To me this includes the twilight of dawn and dusk as well as the brighter light of the noonday sun.

Along the Wild Atlantic Way, County Kerry, Ireland

In fact, I do my best writing in the twilight hours when the creative impulse feels more like mist than crystal.

Ireland's Poetical Atmosphere

My visits to the west coast of Ireland have offered the same misty environment. Here the dynamic interchange between land and sea and sky resounds in perpetual change, while the island's thin places part the veil between material and ethereal dimensions.

Of course, I cannot always physically fly to my soul's home in the Emerald Isle, so I often imagine myself settling into its numinous atmosphere that prompts a poetical frame of mind.

Retaining the receptive mode that Ireland engenders is vital for hearing what my soul wants to convey to me, regardless of where on planet Earth my feet are planted. Being in that space is one of my life's greatest pleasures.

The Joy of Creativeness

Creativeness imbued with Love builds a momentum of inner wisdom that avoids the mere cleverness of the shadow, whose artifacts inevitably contain an element of cruelty and half truth—the ego's lie of material self-sufficiency.

Engaging our creative ability can release tensions we may not have known we were carrying. With every innovation our soul and inner guide draw closer to their permanent bonding. Our desire to be unfettered from limitation increases, and the Wise Inner Counselor extends more of its essence.

This is the joy of creativeness that bathes our best efforts. When we achieve a sublime connection that warms us heart and soul, tears may come in the presence of the Divine's gratitude for our striving to intensify our partnership.

Chapter Twenty-Five

OPENING TO CREATIVENESS

Although poetry is one of my favorite creative expressions, you do not have to be a poet or actor or musician or painter or sculptor or any other traditionally artistic person in order to express creativeness.

Maslow had this point brought home to him in observing his wife's mother. She had very little money and yet she managed to create a beautiful home to which she was always adding touches of color or design.

Watching her put together a simple arrangement of dried grasses caused Maslow to look more deeply into how anyone can express the creativeness that is natural to them and that often produces superior results.

Becoming a Lively Stone

An image comes to mind of the intuitive expertise of a dry stone wall builder from Ireland or Wales.

The master builder knows that each stone contains the perfect shape that will allow it to fit in harmonious relationship with every other piece in the wall. His task is to sense the energy as well as the geometry of the stones so he can nestle them into place where they may remain for centuries without mortar or any other binding agent. Once a stone fits, it stays.

When we deeply connect with our creativeness, we become lively stones in harmony with every other individual the Great

Stonemason has created. The real key is absolute concentration on the matter-in-hand so that distractions disappear and we become one with the task before us.

Dry Stone Wall, Dingle Peninsula, County Kerry, Ireland

Discovering My Creativeness

I remember deciding in elementary school that I would never create anything original. For the rest of my life, I would play only piano pieces written by other people or sing songs that others had composed. I had almost no natural drawing ability, so that clinched the limitation in my mind.

Although I had been given music and dance lessons during much of my childhood, they were always aimed at a recital. Even my personal life felt scripted. Fortunately, pursuing a theater degree in college changed all that.

In an introductory course titled "Integration of Abilities," the fireworks of creative potential exploded in my being. The first assignment was to fabricate a physical metaphor of an emotion or thought. I stayed up all night completing the project and I was on fire. Creativeness was pouring in, through, and around me!

The metaphorical "thing" I made was highly abstract. I do not recall its specific meaning, although at the time I know it did represent a vital truth for my soul.

Creating it was a *Eureka!* moment. I had constructed an artifact that was totally unique. No one else would have assembled some sticks and glue and paint and a piece of bright green translucent plastic in quite the same way.

I felt like dancing—that is, until it came time to present my "creation" in class. Then I had to laugh, because many of my fellow students were just as nervous about showing the strange-looking abstractions they had put together.

The fact that most of us were equally motivated and, in this case, equally unskilled as artists was what mattered. Our instructor's aim was for us to experience crafting something new and previously unexpressed by us personally. Our individual contact with the fire of creativeness was the point.

Opening Up

Improvisation was a main focus of the theater program I attended. I was awkward at first. But after my *Eureka!* experience, I began to open up. I soon discovered that I could be spontaneously funny.

Actually, my inner comedienne had already been poking her head above the surface in high school. This college course was offering even more opportunities to stretch my comedic wings. Now I really was on the road to self-actualization.

Later I would transcend the identity I was forming as an

actor in favor of speaking and writing. But for that very important time in my life, the foundation of true individuality was emerging.

Contacting my innate creativeness in an environment that supported it gave me access to soul gifts that I had never engaged with such clarity or intensity. I was beginning to dance to my own tune—the music of my Wise Inner Counselor.

Things Are Different Now

It is strange to recall how creatively blocked I was as a child. Now I know in my bones that if I do not give voice to my soul's deep desire to create, I will simply expire. I write because I must.

These days I can wax poetical about the liberating power of creativeness. Earlier in my life, discovering how to unlock my personal potential was a battle I am grateful to have won.

Chapter Twenty-Six

Seeking the "Growing Tip"

Although Maslow always identified himself as a scientist, the fact that he zeroed in on the necessity of spirituality and the arts as essential to our being fully human speaks volumes about him as a person. That insight explains why we can learn so much from him about being an innovative self-transcender.

He never stopped exploring, learning, challenging his fears, and staying true to his own values when he was the only one of his colleagues who thought as he did. He relished being known as a Utopian idealist and developed his theories with an eye to creating a better world for future generations.

Maslow really was his work's best exemplar.

Maslow's Creativeness in Action

I recently re-read the introduction to *The Farthest Reaches of Human Nature* that was written by Maslow's good friend Henry Geiger.

If you want an intimate view of the psychologist and the man, I recommend these pages as a lyrically insightful portrait of a trailblazer who "leaps along, sure of his footing," confident in the importance of his mission, and firmly grounded in years of research that proved empirically what he knew intuitively.

Geiger shows us the philosophical scientist who lived in the perpetually transcending world he observed in his subjects. He was always seeking the "growing tip" where change occurs—

where new, more advanced discoveries are constantly emerging in every arena of human endeavor.

Always Striving for Clarity

Maslow was continually coining new terms to express the ineffable qualities he was experiencing in himself and observing in others. This relentless drive for clarity is evident in *The Farthest Reaches* where he offers thirty-five meanings of transcendence in ten-plus pages of very small type.

While watching his two video interviews from 1968, I could see him still reaching for just the right word to explain the concepts that were clear to him because he lived them, but that were not always clear to others. Or that were incompletely or incorrectly interpreted by those who lacked his vision.

He was wordsmithing in real time, refining language to better express an idea that still resisted the full definition he sought, even after years of research, writing, and lecturing.

A remarkable thing Maslow said about his writing and speaking was that his real audience was actually comprised of his own exemplars of self-transcendence—Socrates, Spinoza, and others. He did his best to stay out of what he called "the journalistic world" and remain in the eternal world. He was always thinking of his great-great-grandchildren as those who might truly receive his message.

Nurturing Innate Creativeness

Maslow had a lot of say about nurturing the inborn creativeness of children, which he believed would naturally lead to their self-actualization. He is at his most idealistic when describing his concept of enlightened education. He also sounds like a teacher of the Montessori Method.

When Maslow writes that the goal of education should be the self-actualization of all students by supporting their development into the best they can become, Dr. Maria Montessori would have agreed.

As one of Italy's first female physicians, her early medical practice focused on psychiatry. Later she became interested in childhood education, notably for those with learning disabilities. Her observations and experiments to determine the most effective methods produced admirable results and led to her opening a childcare center in a poor, underserved area of Rome.

Montessori's First Classroom

Maslow would have loved that the children, who were unruly at first, soon became fascinated by Montessori's activities that tapped into their natural desire to learn. In a short time they were highly absorbed in the materials from which they were free to choose. That "choosing" led them into deep concentration and natural self-discipline.

Montessori's trust in the children's inner teacher fostered their ability to absorb knowledge from the light-filled classroom environment that allowed their inner genius to lead them toward what was most important for their individual advancement.

The Freedom to Learn

Maslow called this "intrinsic education," which creates an environment that gives children, and the young adults he taught, the freedom to learn about themselves, their preferences and talents, and what they are *not* suited for in terms of vocation.

He said this approach leads to the cognition of Being and the intrinsic Being-values that his subjects reported as central to actualizing their full potential.

Joyful Total Absorption

This is the child-centered education that Montessori spent her life developing. She designed materials that kindled the children's natural creativeness as they engaged in the serious, concentrated play of learning.

Maslow's descriptions of his subjects' full attention to the matter-in-hand reflected the same kind of joyful, total absorption that Montessori's students demonstrated in their complete engagement with their lessons.

Had these two trailblazers ever met, I can imagine them talking non-stop for days. They would be excitedly discussing the positive effects their methods produced in students and their teachers who functioned less like instructors and more like Maslow's supportive, non-interfering helpers.

I can hear these two geniuses agreeing on the necessity of intrinsic education so the growing tip of creativeness can be experienced at any time of life, in a multitude of situations.

As their conversations ranged far into the night, I also can imagine them sharing their personal experiences with the inner teacher that inspired their innovations. While observing them, anyone who had eyes to see such things would likely have noticed a mystical glow emanating from these two illumined beings.

Creativeness in Collaboration

A dynamic I have noticed in my own life is how merely being in the same physical space with others who are absorbed in their own projects has a way of creating new sparks of illumination for everyone in the room.

Likewise, consciously joining forces with others adds to the joy of innovation. There is nothing quite like sharing the sense of accomplishment when a group project is successfully completed.

Collaboration is one of the activities I loved most about my career as an actor and singer. Although sometimes very challenging, the shared creativity of rehearsals was frequently a lot of fun—especially when I was working with other entertainers who were generous with their ideas and open to mine. When we got to show time, the synergy we had developed made for some great performances.

What I have realized only recently is that the audience also became active collaborators in the live event. They might arrive feeling burdened by any number of circumstances. Our job as performers was to lift their spirits, which often lifted our own.

Sometimes magic happened, in part, I believe, because the spirit of creativeness was ignited in the souls of every person who was present for that show. During the space of two or three hours, we were collectively engaged in total absorption—the growing tip where resistance flees and inner light comes to life.

Chapter Twenty-Seven

Actualizing Our Creativeness

I have found that increasing my creativeness depends on expanding my receptivity. There is a tremendous amount of "allowing" involved in receiving the flashes of inspiration which then can be fleshed out into entire works.

I become aware of my soul responding to the presence of my Wise Inner Counselor. That contact feels like an invitation to engage more meditatively in co-creating, as if innovation exists between the visible and invisible dimensions of daily life.

Accessing Other Realms

Seen and unseen planes are both known to the soul, although not to the extent that the Wise Inner Counselor is aware of material and etheric dimensions. What the soul cannot readily access is the realm of the Eternal One who does not descend to time and space.

Every once in a while the etheric plane does make itself known through peak experiences that enliven the soul with visions of numinous dimensions which emanate cosmic unity. These illuminations can make our outer consciousness more receptive to the intimations of inner guidance.

Ways to Think About Transcendence

I sometimes think we are all a bit like Pinocchio, who wanted to be a real boy. Our soul longs to be one with the True Self, to merge with that marvelous realm of mystical Being.

To reach that goal, the inner guide uses our imagination to show us how life could be. We become the hero in our own drama, victoriously slaying the dragon of the shadow self.

Another way to think of creativeness is as a scaffolding or framework through which the Wise Inner Counselor conveys all of the values of Being. It is through our unique gifts that we are able to transform those values into virtues. This is where the sacred labor becomes a vehicle for transcending the egoic self.

Creativeness can nurture an expression of transcendence that is highly experiential. It can involve the full unification of being and doing into a more refined stage of development. In this new way of living, the soul fully participates in the matter-in-hand with no reservation, doubt, or sense of separateness.

Bringing Novelty into the World

Creativeness functions in us as the very core of self-transcendence. While peak experiences may inspire new levels of awareness and greater desire for transcendence as a unitive way of life, our soul ability to bring something novel into the world is how we actualize our potential as complete humans.

As you may have observed in your own life, self-actualization involves much more than finding the perfect job where you can do what you like. It is a matter of bringing the essence of your capabilities into whatever occupation may be paying your bills.

When I did personal coaching using a model that identified my clients' thinking style preferences, I learned that any job can be an expression of your creativeness. The key is to notice what of your talents are coming to the fore or which ones can be more fully expressed, even in a job you may not prefer.

Sadly, not all people are inspired to exceed the obstacles of psychology that may appear in the unhealthy stories they have been revolving around their life experience.

Yet I am convinced that a positive, creative environment can work wonders. I saw that happen many times when I was a professional development instructor.

The Healing Power of Creative Play

During the leadership academy that I facilitated for two years, I witnessed how games that stimulated creative problem-solving eased longstanding animosities between some of the participants.

When I taught assertiveness skills, the course author and I wrote funny role-play scenarios that prompted students to practice various techniques. I laughed and watched in amazement as many shy individuals who had come to class seriously lacking in self-esteem departed with confidence in their ability to respond effectively to challenging situations and aggressive co-workers.

Gaining a Feeling of Certainty

We contain within us the seeds of our own transcendence—the inner force of creativeness that impels us forward and that may play a part in attracting peak experiences of universal unity.

The transfiguring power of those peaks infuses our illumined consciousness with a certainty that translates into trust in the possibility of exceeding the limited self. In these moments of conversion, our motivation increases for continuing to learn and grow and innovate.

In deep communion with our inherent creativeness, we become messengers for the cosmic consciousness of our True Self. We give utterance to that awareness through our words and deeds. And our spirits soar.

Chapter Twenty-Eight

SPIRALS OF CREATIVENESS

I hear the word "spiral" used frequently. I use it myself. When I consider the word's significance in relation to self-transcendence, images from Nature come to mind.

A spiral begins in the compressed seed of a plant, an idea, a person, or a project. The potential for reaching great heights exists as the blueprint of a mighty oak, fully contained in the humble acorn. Intelligence resides in the seed, needing only soil, sun, water, and a place in which to expand unfettered.

I like the example of how fern fronds uncoil from tightly wound to fully extended. Watching time lapse videos of plants growing shows how Nature nurtures her spirals—from seedling to bud to full blossom to myriad new seeds at season's end.

Spirals Everywhere

It was on my first visit to Ireland that I became aware of how frequently the ancients used this symbol—like the swirling images carved into the massive entrance stone at Newgrange, a neolithic monument of spiritual significance that is over 5,000 years old.

After that encounter, I began seeing spirals everywhere!

Creativeness Is in Our Bones

We humans are highly inventive idea generators. We are perpetually initiating new energetic bursts of inspiration that zoom out into the world like a quarterback's perfect pass.

We delight in co-creating with the Divine. We can't help ourselves. Creativeness is in our bones.

And how do flashes of inspiration come to us? Just like a compact fern frond, the flash of an idea may arrive as a kernel of a plan—a *Eureka!* image that can be uncoiled and expanded. The process unfolds, almost as if a cosmic blueprint already exists for how we are meant to transform what's now into what's next.

Miraculous Staircase, Loretto Chapel, Santa Fe, New Mexico

An Ideal Image

I usually think of blueprints as linear, two-dimensional representations of what will become three dimensional. But what if the soul's blueprint is a multi-dimensional spiral like the miraculous Loretto Chapel staircase in Santa Fe, New Mexico?[43]

Meditating on the impeccable symmetry of its thirty-three steps and double-helix shape draws the eye up, inspiring the soul to reach higher. There is no visible center pole around which the stairs curve. And yet there is a forcefield of energy inherent in the perfect geometry that allows the structure to support its own weight and hold its shape.

Perhaps this is an ideal image that the Divine envisions as we make our way through myriad trials and triumphs on our voyage to Eternity. Within the spiral are steps of opportunity that unfold naturally as we climb, urged on by an inner desire to achieve with each revolution a higher degree of enlightenment, psychological health, and Being-consciousness.

Evolving Perspectives

The Loretto staircase is a useful metaphor for demonstrating how this geometry functions within the spiritual journey. Each step includes and transcends our prior attainment. Progress rests upon the foundation of what we have previously transformed.

While climbing the staircase, we gain a 360-degree view of our surroundings. Each time we come around to the same outer view, we are higher up on the steps. The scene shifts and the opportunities for progress change.

We may frequently find ourselves returning to similar life circumstances involving a karmic obligation that has not been fully transmuted. With each revolution of the cosmic spiral, we may discover means for handling that situation from a more evolved perspective. When we apply greater love, wisdom, faith, determination, compassion, and hope than the last time we visited this curve in the path, we can arrive at new points of reference and often a felt sense that life is becoming more luminous.

Sequence or Great Leaps?

Like the chambered nautilus, much of the natural world grows in geometrical shapes that develop with mathematical precision. Nature does not skip steps, though people do. Or so it may seem.

To the great consternation of parents, employers, friends, lovers, and colleagues who expect us to continue unchanged in situations and relationships to which they have become accustomed, self-transcenders are inveterate spiral-leapers.

We are perpetually scouting the horizon for the next step on life's helical staircase. We may have earned a reputation for quitting projects or jobs about which we had been very enthusiastic. However, the likely truth is that we have integrated all we could learn from that situation. For us, that cycle is complete. We see little reason to devote more energy to a circumstance that no longer supports our creative thinking or encourages us to grow.

To others (and sometime to ourselves) our journey through life may appear less like an orderly chambered nautilus and more like moths flying around a streetlight. We are also attracted to the light and the route we take to get there may be equally circuitous.

As our perspectives evolve, we may find ourselves negotiating multiple spirals that are all turning simultaneously and differently, depending upon our various roles, relationships, jobs, and hobbies—even our beliefs.

Some cycles are short-term while others last longer. Some are visible and others operate invisibly at inner levels that we may sense only occasionally. Each unfolds in its own time, ideally leaving us more illumined than we were in the past.

Seizing the Day

I am grateful that spiritual forces have occasionally intervened in my life, usually to save me from myself. Although benign, those interventions often have felt like electrical shocks that propelled me onto an entirely new trajectory of soul growth.

Such dramatic changes could be called mercy or grace or good luck or a major challenge. Whatever term I use to identify them, they have seemed to dissolve the final turn of a cycle that may involve my learning lessons, paying spiritual or monetary debts, or being introduced to new opportunities.

Although these sudden shocks may appear like magic, my sense is that they occur because I have completed an obligation that I actually may not have been aware of. They are a bit like the "overnight successes" that result from many years of hard work.

In any case, my task is to seize the day. Leap to the next step on the cosmic staircase and make the most of it.

What If We Fall Off?

I agree with the old adage that if you can't make a mistake, you can't make anything. I also have learned that if I am going to make a mistake, I should try for a new one. That's progress.

Sometimes Spirit's interventions look a lot like mistakes when they knock me off a staircase I have been merrily climbing. However, I can honestly say that the shocks, fails, losses, and sorrows that appear to have wiped out past achievements or concepts of who I am have been the making of me.

Life in the Non-Linear

Sequential or linear time is a system that works well as long as we adhere to it. But anyone who has suffered great loss will tell you that when all of that seeming regularity is disrupted, your awareness of linear time goes out the window.

Life suddenly feels chaotic. Your sense of order turns into swoops and swirls of emotion and altered perceptions of the world and your place in it. Your thoughts may start looping around like moths seeking the light.

Living through the primal nature of grief that follows loss showed me the possibility that twists, turns, loops, curves, and waves are how life fundamentally operates.

Grief can open a portal to etheric realms that are more real than what we perceive here in the physical. Perhaps Reality is actually composed of a non-linear geometry of energy patterns that offer a different perspective on how creativeness authentically emerges.

If that is the case, then Nature's fondness for spirals may hold clues to how we can engage our native creativeness with inner guidance to surf the waves of life's tumultuous challenges that invariably involve loss.

Chapter Twenty-Nine

CREATIVENESS IN LOSS

We usually do not associate creativeness with loss and grief. But I can tell you with a certainty that creativeness was my lifeline to survival after Stephen died.

He had been sick for two years, but was fully expected to beat the cancer that seemed like an anomaly for a healthy, robust man in his early fifties. However, when the disease returned a year after treatment, the diagnosis was "not curable."

The Sunday after we received the news that no one wants to hear, we parked our car near a restaurant where we planned to have breakfast. The entire front range of the Colorado Rocky Mountains spread out before us with springtime snows still dusting some of the tallest peaks.

As I gazed at this glorious view of eternal grandeur, I had a vision of a commission for the two of us. Stephen's part was to go on across the veil between worlds. Mine was to stay and tell our story. We had already decided that if anyone could face the heartbreak of losing each other, we could. This vision gave me the tools for surviving and eventually for thriving.

Writing My Way to Selfhood

Over the fifteen years since Stephen has been gone, I have literally written my way into my True Self. I continue to discover deeper and wider inner landscapes and fountains of resilience that I certainly did not perceive immediately after my beloved passed from this world to the next.

Immersing myself in compiling into a book the hundreds of journal pages I had written in the final two-and-a-half years of Stephen's life became my reason for being. And while I was writing, my communion with his spirit grew stronger, as did my connection with my Wise Inner Counselor.

My Mother Was a Great Example

When my father passed away ten years before Stephen's departure, my mother, Pauline, attended a course for widowed persons that was conducted by her church's associate minister who held a master's degree in psychology.

Pauline had always enjoyed doing a bit of writing, so I was not really surprised that she eagerly participated in the journaling exercises the minister suggested. I was living in Littleton, Colorado, and she was in Sun City, Arizona, so I was not privy to her experience. What I did observe was the result.

During the several weeks of this course, my sweet mama profoundly internalized her fifty-seven years of marriage to my father. When I saw her next, she told me, "Dennis is here in my heart and I know I will not lose him."

Sun City is known as a city of volunteers, so there were multiple opportunities for Pauline to get involved in a wide range of activities. Also, her friends were trying to set her up with a number of widowers from their church. But my mom held firm. She said to me, "I don't want to do what my friends think I should. I want to do what my heart tells me."

Not only did my mother not lose the essence of my father's spirit that was now safely abiding in her heart, she also was able to open to a new love with a man whose family and ours had been friends for over twenty-five years.

Her creative journaling practice had put her firmly in touch with her Wise Inner Counselor, so she was confident in following the inner guidance that led her to Ken.

After they were married (at the age of 81!), Pauline took up watercolor painting, which gave her a way of expressing her talent for creating beauty in her person and surroundings. Several years later that creative outlet helped see her through Ken's stroke and her own deteriorating health.

I just now realized that I never saw her journal pages. She must have destroyed them after they had served their purpose. I do the same. Creative integration is what matters. My mother was a great example of how that can work in loss.

Creative Familiarity with the Unknown

Stephen's mother, Marie, was a talented weaver and textile artist. She produced large wall hangings and smaller tapestries that expressed how she cherished her family and her own creativity.

Losing her middle son was extremely traumatic for her, especially because Stephen was very private about his spiritual journey with dying. We both preferred that I be his only caregiver. With his parents living an hour away, this arrangement was easier. But not being with him daily was hard for his family.

After Stephen was gone, Marie and I had many intimate conversations that helped us both come to terms with our loss. We frequently talked about our creative projects. She was weaving a new series of tapestries and I was writing my memoir.

We learned a lot from each other. And we agreed that our already being familiar with the unknowns that are central to any creative activity actually helped us when life forced us into the Great Unknown of the mystery of life and death.

Walking Through the Healing Portal

I often have shared the examples of these two mothers as a way to encourage others to listen for promptings that may suggest a creative activity that can become a portal to their innermost reality.

An important key I learned from Maslow is that we achieve the greatest benefit from any activity when we engage our full attention. When we focus on the matter-in-hand with all of our heart, mind, and soul, we may enter a timeless, unselfconscious zone where the concerns of the lesser self do not exist.

When our intention is centered on expressing whatever our soul wants to bring into the world, we walk through the portal of the heart into the domain of the Wise Inner Counselor where healing can happen.

The Divine Answers Before We Ask

I have filled three books[44] and countless articles with the many lessons I have learned about loss and grief, and about how the presence of our innate creativeness can lead to unexpected instances of lasting joy.

Every time I approach the subject, I gain deeper insight into the healing power of this inborn faculty that the Divine placed in our souls in anticipation of the day when we would cry out for a lifeline.

Through the rough waters of loss that likely will be ours to navigate at some time in our life, the answer already exists. We need only reach out and take hold of the gift of creativeness that can see us through the darkest hours.

Chapter Thirty

Our Soul's Greatest Creation

I am convinced that our greatest creation is a relationship of trust and cooperation with our Wise Inner Counselor. Our soul is meant to reflect the Eternal, yet we often need reminding by our inner guide about how to achieve that transformation.

Our souls are burdened by karma, by toxins in the body and surrounding environment, by mental confusion that muffles the voice of Wisdom. While our True Self fights for the soul, our soul must fight for that indwelling presence who has difficulty penetrating a dense body or unreceptive heart.

As long as we inhabit a body, we have an opportunity to liberate our soul by balancing karma and fulfilling our reason for being. When life ends and we return to etheric octaves, we feel the joy of release from the material plane, but we are not free. Our soul cannot escape the wheel of reembodiment without help.

Sometimes that help comes in the form of like-minded sojourners who are traveling the same journey of transcendence.

Soul Synchronicity

In his enchanting memoir, *The Candle of Vision,* Irish mystic George W. Russell describes how he found the kindred souls we may identify as his fellow transcenders.

As a teenager, Æ (his pen name) began to have peak experiences which convinced him that he was living surrounded by a golden age. The visions were ephemeral, leaving him to wonder if the paradise he had entered would ever come again.

To his delight, the visions continued. And Æ noticed that "every intense imagination, every new adventure of the intellect [was] endowed with magnetic power to attract to it, its own kin." In other words, he began to meet other people who were mystics. He called them his "intimates of the spirit."[45]

Spiritual Gravitation

In Æ's novel *The Avatars,* several of the characters discuss their encounter with the same experience. Those who are like them in soul essence are drawn into their sphere of acquaintance. They call this effect "spiritual gravitation."

I found this description highly synchronistic. In the last year of Stephen's life, he frequently spoke about invoking light to create the "spiritual gravity" that would draw his soul straight up to etheric planes when he passed.

My impression is that the gravitational pull of spiritual light operates horizontally in the material plane to attract people, circumstances, and resources that are necessary for our mission in time and space. And it functions vertically to draw us to Spirit and Spirit to us for the ultimate liberation of our souls.

We Attract Who We Are

We not only teach who we are, we attract to ourselves energies similar to those we project out into the world. That is how we ultimately find our transcendent companions.

Looking back on my life, I can see how that truth played out with great precision. The circumstances in which I found myself were a direct outpicturing of my attitudes. When my thoughts and feelings were prompted by rebellion against some aspect of life, I drew to myself other rebellious people. At the same time, when I payed attention to the still small voice of my Wise Inner Counselor, life flowed along quite smoothly.

Æ's insights explained to me why I was attracted to the spiritual journey that he says is open to everyone, though few actually choose it. He says, "It is a path within ourselves."

And, fortunately, we are graced with assistance, both human and divine.

Our Good Karma
We may encounter true helpers who rescue us from doldrums and confusion. They may quite literally pull us out of the mud. I am convinced that one reason they can render this selfless aid is that we have done the same for others in the past, and all souls enjoy returning the favor.

The spiritual journey may awaken in us for any number of reasons. Perhaps desperation brings about true surrender to a will that is greater than our own. Perhaps we have walked this path many times before and in this life we have the opportunity to come full circle.

What About Art?
In light of Æ's restorative sojourns to the picturesque shores of County Donegal, Ireland, where for several weeks nearly every summer he painted pictures of his ethereal visions, I began to ponder what role art might play in nurturing a luminous life.

I recalled how years ago I was treating myself to an art walk through a number of small, niche galleries that were promoting the work of local artists. Upon entering an obscure gallery located on a narrow alley, I happened upon a heated discussion between several people who were debating the purpose of art.

All agreed that art began as the expression of the artist's

individual perception of some aspect of their outer or inner world. But to what ultimate purpose? Was inspiring and uplifting an audience the reason for art, or was art meant only to evoke a reaction from those who experience it, without regard for positive or negative effects?

I knew where I stood. For me all of the arts are meant to illumine and elevate the audience. Apparently that was not the intention of this particular exhibit. The paintings, sculptures, carvings, ceramics, and metalwork all featured jagged shapes, grotesque images, and garish colors that definitely produced in me an immediate response.

My head began to ache. I became dizzy and nauseous. Despite the host's inviting buffet of snacks and beverages, I made a quick exit in favor of fresh air, blue skies, and bright sunshine.

I went home after that experience and thought a lot about why I write. One of the most important reasons is that I do want to make a positive difference in the world.

My hope is that whatever I create will radiate out to others in a way that kindles in them a light of the eternal verities of all that is true and good and beautiful about themselves.

From reading the works of Æ, I know he would agree.

A Mystic's Gratitude

Words stream softly
in the misty morn
and stories fall gently from the sky.

When space is cleared
and kindness given,
the heavens open to greater gifts;
the best of all—creativeness.

Here is true worship.
Devotion to one's art
is communion, indeed.

No need for physical ritual
or remembrance.
In these moments
light essence
is transferred directly.

For here is truth made manifest
in the lover of words
whose only desire
is to hear what Spirit speaks
and fasten that missive to paper
on behalf of a future
the Eternal One might bless.

Chapter Thirty-One

Reflecting on Your Luminous Life - 4

I invite you to listen as your heart opens to creativeness, and the fragrance of your soul's essence makes itself known as radiant, unlimited possibility. Fresh insights into the deeper aspects of your own authentic Self may surprise you in these musings.

Feel free to honor them with a response, or rest in the void that can be the richest tribute of all. And as you reflect, may you experience the oneness that exists between all dimensions of your being.

Be Spacious in Your Contemplation
Giving yourself plenty of time for this exercise is a lovely way to relax into contemplation. These interior connections contain their own spaceless timelessness that may take a while to emerge.

We cannot force *aha!* moments to appear. Still, we can develop an environment of receptivity that welcomes the light in which creativeness thrives.

Sometimes that is the most fun.

Part Five

Strengthening the Thread of Contact

*The seen needs the Unseen
to prove the reality
of conversation
that feeds
the flame of Self.*

Chapter Thirty-Two

To Live in Wonder

I am reminded of a wise saying that "the pearl is invisible in the depths."[46] Reality in the unitive experience is not obvious from the external. To answer Spirit's call to live as my True Self, I feel my awareness easing into the realm of mystical Being where the mind is visionary and the heart is a perceiver of eternal verities.

The following chapters emerged from my contemplation of mysteries that came to light when I let the mystical teach me about itself.

Into the Ineffable

The farther up the spiral of Being we climb, the more difficult describing the ascent may become. Thoughts, images, impressions arrive in fragments. The veil between dream and waking thins, and we may not have a clear idea of which realm is which.

Perception changes moment to moment. Vision clarifies and delight in existence increases as a world of wonder offers its own form of self-transcendence. Love becomes the ocean in which we swim as both source and motivation for our continuing journey into the ineffable.

A Deepening Partnership

On the ascent we discover a deepening partnership with Spirit that swoops and spins and swirls in perpetual surprise, shining a light on myriad aspects of consciousness.

Because we yet inhabit the plane of time and space with its inherent limitations on our ability to perceive the unity of all intrinsic values at once, each turn of the spiral offers a richer view of previous steps on the cosmic stairway.

The farther we climb, the tests become more subtle and perhaps more easily failed, though Love has answered before we think to ask. Our full attention to the present moment opens the door to each new phase of Being.

As our accelerating consciousness allows the Wise Inner Counselor greater proximity to our soul, our receptivity to the eternal verities increases.

We find ourselves displacing residual elements of the artificial self and filling in the voids with compassion, wisdom, and strength—the very qualities we need to continue ascending the spiral of Being.

E Pluribus Unum

Why do I refer to a single spiral when transcending the conditioned self appears to involve our negotiating multiple illumined pathways?

As my life on this journey has evolved, I have found that insights about diverse concepts begin coalescing into a central theme of attunement with divine guidance. Out of many spirals one eventually emerges, although the final consummation may not occur until countless cycles have come to fruition.

A friend once showed me a photograph that was taken of a very spiritual woman shortly before her passing. Winding around her entire body from below her feet to far above the top of her head was a perfectly symmetrical coil of milky-white energy.

Perhaps this is what the spiral of Being actually looks like.

Attuning to Spiritual Timelines

While living our lives in the visible world, what we are called to transmute in order to attain the goal of our own brilliant coil of ascending energy will be unique to each of us, as will the outcomes we achieve.

One of the results I am already observing in my voyage to the unitive is clearer perception of cycles and a stronger ability to meet the spiritual timelines that I sense are intensifying.

Myriad tasks are calling to be accomplished amidst periods of rest and vital conversations. All the while I am prompted to strengthen the thread of contact with my Wise Inner Counselor to complete what is mine to fulfill.

There is a crystalline quality to this intuition. I liken it to cleaning my car's windshield or polishing a mirror so it more clearly reflects the images arrayed before it.

I recently looked at myself in a mirror and realized that I had changed. Something unnecessary had dropped away. I was more of my genuine Self in that moment than I had been the day before. As long as I continue communing with inner guidance, I trust that I will have the same experience many times before my journey is through.

This truly is living in Wonder.

Chapter Thirty-Three

A Passion for the Summit

The Great Lights of history have demonstrated an undying passion for their mission. Even when assailed as dangerous, crazy, criminal, or heretical, they have held to their convictions.

These are the individuals that history remembers because they were the pioneers, the relentless self-transcenders who were never content, even with their latest breakthroughs.

The Inner Fire Leads Us

Although the world may do its worst to thwart us, like these trailblazers we honor the connection with our inner guide. We hold fast to our intrinsic values. We do not interfere with the promptings of our heart. And we do not contort our behavior to match an artificial construct of what is acceptable to a synthetic society.

We allow the fire in our hearts to lead us. We are not attached to the fruits of our labors, though neither are we oblivious to the consequences of our actions or inactions. If our thoughts, words, and deeds are not bearing good fruit, we change.

Desiring the Ascension

Each new phase of transcendence is often preceded by a burning in the heart that impels us forward, convincing us that we may no longer rest at the level we have reached.

We may begin to feel a certain dryness, a sensation that saints of old called "aridity." In this state we feel as if our insides have become a desert. We long for an oasis to refresh our soul and replenish our inner resources.

I have experienced that aridity in my own life. There have been times when I have felt a longing building in my soul, but my projects were not moving forward as I thought they should.

I found myself at the edge of another cycle of creativeness, but that spiral did not seem to be turning. I could tell that I was evolving beyond my former state of consciousness, but I was in that transition space that feels like a never-ending middle of nowhere.

Over the years I have learned that increasing my love for the matter-in-hand is the way through. Inevitably, the apparent lack of forward movement is an invitation for me to go deeper, to release any preconceived notions, to listen with greater receptivity, and to let Spirit work through me. (Or on me.)

Transcendence Simply Is

To transcend is to be continually filled with longing for the deeper depths, the higher heights, the holier holies of consciousness that our Wise Inner Counselor assures us do exist.

All the while we are one hundred percent in ecstatic love with the astounding experience of being here, embodied on planet Earth at this period of history where today's illumination is the only one of its kind that ever was or ever will be again.

Transcendence is a mystery that no one can fully explain, no matter how many studies or theories are written. To transcend is to live the mystery. To love enough to risk the outer life for the interior one. To give up all pretense of egoic accomplishment or need to prove our worthiness to a materialistic world.

The only true legacy is Love. And the only real Love is found in complete absorption in this moment and in the next and the next. Transcendence simply *is* and so we are perpetually transcending.

Kindling Our Passion Anew

As our soul's reunion with the Infinite draws near, we may feel a profound yearning, a longing, a desire to increase those sublime moments of inner communion. And then suddenly the Divine presence becomes too much to bear.

Our heart expands and our body weeps. Tears flow in a sensation that is too vast to contain. Too exquisite to describe. And yet, too wonderful not to share, lest we fail to internalize this bliss by forgetting why we live and why we must go on living until that final instant of luminous transformation occurs—a moment that we can neither prophesy nor anticipate.

The nearness of the Eternal can produce chills, a tingling energy that is scintillating, almost like our bloodstream is filled with champagne that bubbles from the base of our spine to the top of our crown chakra.

Such a concentration of Love cannot be retained for long. We begin to feel as if our body may simply give way because our vessel is too small, too weak. So, Spirit recedes a bit, temporarily lessening its proximity, offering our soul an opportunity to assimilate the experience, and then to welcome more light. To desire the next wave of Love.

To embrace the exquisite pain of the soul's longing for reunion is to enter the mystery of Being. For when our soul gains insight into the hunger that cannot be satisfied by anything in this world, fresh vistas open into the liminal and our passion for the summit is kindled anew.

Afternoon sun reflecting on the Pacific Ocean near Carmel, California

Chapter Thirty-Four

MIRROR OF THE OVER-SOUL

The divine spark that lives in our heart of hearts is a reflection of our Highest Self, the Eternal One. We are a drop of the cosmic ocean that is equal to the entire ocean.

The quality is the same. Only quantity is different. And even then, if we could enter fully into the consciousness of the True Self, we would find ourselves instantly expanded into the Infinite.[47]

Emerson's Perception

Emerson seems to have understood this equation when he wrote in his essay *The Over-Soul*:

> Meantime within man is the soul of the whole; the wise silence; the universal beauty, to which every part and particle is equally related; the eternal ONE.

When I first read *The Over-Soul*, I was puzzled by how Emerson sometimes sounds as if he is speaking from the presence of inner divinity and at other times he is speaking from the higher atmosphere of the Infinite.

Now I realize that during his meditation that prompted this essay, he was in the flow of energy moving back and forth between the two. The Sage of Concord, as he was affectionately known, would have perceived no separation because, in reality, there is none.

Yet Separation Remains

All of these elements exist within us. The fact that we may consider ourselves separate from our Divine Self is astonishing. And yet, we do.

Early in *The Over-Soul* Emerson himself acknowledges that when he perceives the "ethereal water" of inspiration that flows to him from unseen sources, he feels like "a pensioner; not a cause, but a surprised spectator." Then he elaborates with these sublime words:

> I dare not speak for it. My words do not carry its august sense; they fall short and cold. Only itself can inspire whom it will and behold! their speech shall be lyrical and sweet....Yet I desire, even by profane words, if I may not use sacred, to indicate the heaven of this deity and to report what hints I have collected of the transcendent simplicity and energy of the Highest Law.[48]

Becoming Lovers of Language

So, how do we bridge the gap in consciousness between our human mind and the Over-Soul? I believe one answer is to become inspired practitioners of language, as did Emerson—whom Æ avidly credited with "the healthiest mind of America."[49]

Like Emerson and Æ, many prominent transcenders have been lovers of language who wrote and spoke from the profound inspiration of luminous dimensions. Great avatars of all ages have contacted the spiritual Logos behind the words they delivered and have embodied that Word to their followers.

When we are attuned to our Wise Inner Counselor, we may make contact with the same ethereal majesty. Yet despite our best efforts, we may find ourselves earth-bound by our habitual limitations. A major barrier to our contacting the Word behind even the most beautifully written or spoken language may be a subtle doubt in our own soul's native magnificence.

Overcoming Doubt

I have read that doubt in the spark of recognition that originally ignited our desire to pursue the spiritual life is a challenge we may face as advanced voyagers who have been on this journey for many years.

I witnessed this in someone very close to me. Uncertainty that began as subtle questions grew to nearly overwhelming proportions in his mind and came close to derailing him. He has since recovered and commented to me that it was as if doubt had built a wall of resistance to Spirit around his consciousness with a potency he did not detect until it was almost too late.

My friend recently noticed a subtle reticence in me.

"Stop questioning the presence of Spirit," he declared. "This journey to the Infinite is real!"

I could feel the intensity of his words burning shards of doubt out of my entire being.

Attaining Our Birthright

Since this experience, I am doubly convinced that when we surrender our limiting mindsets and consign our false self to the spiritual fires of transmutation, we may receive direct connection with the inner divinity that is our birthright.

We are meant to inherit the perennial wisdom promised to every generation by history's Great Lights. When we strive for that attainment, in the sublime essence of unitive consciousness where separation is resolved, we discover new levels of Selfhood in the wholeness that Emerson encountered as the Over-Soul, the Eternal One.

Chapter Thirty-Five

The Right to Be Divine

As I have studied the works of historical and contemporary mystics, I have discovered a band of revolutionaries. Each in his or her own way was determined to change the world for the betterment of humanity.

These pioneers believed in the right of the individual to be fully human. Ultimately, that meant the right to be divine—to make direct contact with a presence greater than the mundane self and to be fully unified with the Wise Inner Counselor.

To these revolutionaries, entering into the mystery of Self also meant being free to pursue one's calling. This is a sentiment that Wordsworth whole-heartedly advocated as he launched the poetry of personal experience into the English language.

Saint Teresa of Avila was another vigorous self-transcender who followed her own star. She was a fiery soul who lived life to the full as a nun, abbess, founder of monasteries, and creator of a new Carmelite order in her native Spain. She was also a prolific writer of prose, an ecstatic poet, and a spontaneous composer of devotional songs.

What Does Our Future Portend?

We who are living in the twenty-first century have the opportunity to continue where mystic revolutionaries have journeyed before us by pursuing a practical spirituality that encompasses and promotes psychological health.

So, where exactly do we go from here in that pursuit? When I asked my Wise Inner Counselor that question, the answer that reverberated through my whole body was: "Up!" We go up in vibration to the self-transcendence that leads to the unitive.

We have a right to express our innate divinity through our humanity, and we are the only ones who can actualize that right for ourselves. Our goal is the freedom to be authentic, to love life, to be responsible citizens who raise up a good society that is so strong in its positive values that the shadow has no place to hide.

We are not meant to endlessly revolve on the wheel of karma. We are born to ascend out of this plane of illusion into the radiant center of the Eternal One where greater opportunities for service await us. However, to achieve the goal of celestial reunion, we must fulfill certain obligations attached to being human.

Repaying Our Debts

We all have longstanding debts that we did not pay in a former life. Perhaps we died too soon. Or we did not recognize the errors of our ways because our habitual patterns were too ingrained.

Perhaps we received mercy to try again in our next life and we did balance a certain amount of karma, though not all. Or we forgot the promises we made to the masters of wisdom between lives, and we repeated the same old mistakes, yet again.

Whatever the reason, the karma for missing the mark of our self-mastery has come due. Fortunately, we have access to the violet flame, the cosmic regenerator that can eradicate those old patterns of consciousness, personality, and behavior.

Transmutation is the ultimate self-transcendence.

Three Ways of Being Divine

The sixteenth-century mystic Saint John of the Cross and his close friend Teresa of Avila lived profoundly spiritual lives that exemplified the mystical union of the soul with the Divine.

They wrote vividly about their experiences so that others might understand their own pilgrimage to the unitive. These mysteries are not easily understood, although the saints did their best to help us learn from their example.

I recently came upon a teaching from Saint John[50] that I would like to include here. Reading about his three ways of what he called "spiritual exercise" helped me understand a phenomenon that has occurred in my life many times during the past several years.

Saint John's essential three ways are purgative, illuminative, and unitive. Placing them in the context of self-transcendence, they can be described as follows:

- Purgative—the state of beginners, which may include a fair amount of inner and outer correction.
- Illuminative—the state of those who have gained a certain intimacy of understanding through overcoming many obstacles to their self-transcendence.
- Unitive—the state where the aspiring soul achieves union with the True Self in a spiritual chamber of the heart, hidden from all but those with the refined awareness that perceives this profound mystery.

The Spiral Turns Many Times

Although Saint John appears to present his ways as a one-time process, my experience is that the first two spiritual exercises will repeat many times as we ascend the spiral of Being.

When I am working on a new book I go through periods of intense purgation. These are intervals of deep soul searching that include the need for a lot of transmutation and reconsideration of what I actually mean to say.

When I have found my way through a necessary level of the purgative process, my Wise Inner Counselor shines a light on the next phase of writing, which allows me to understand much subtler concepts. And each fresh perspective then clears patterns in my consciousness that could block the flow to a new level of comprehension.

Rather than viewing purgation and illumination as two disparate activities, I see them as complements that are intricately intertwined like a pair of ballroom dancers waltzing in time to the heartbeat of the Universe. The heightened perception, which results from my removing impediments to insight then penetrating deeper into essential meaning, generates the energy that opens a portal to the unitive.

Here is the heart of Saint John's three ways of being divine—in actuality, a multi-faceted process that leads to the unitive and then continues as the dynamic, ongoing transcendence which I have come to realize occurs within the realm of mystical Being. Transformation never ends.

Seeking the Unitive

Is the unitive state too lofty for us to attempt in this modern age? I do not think so. Neither do the numberless mystics who, even today, willingly enter in to Saint John's "spiritual exercise" as a way of living that sustains the vibrancy of their cosmic consciousness.

I am certain we can be counted among them. Wherever we are in the Universe, I feel our fellow travelers cheering us on. For the transcendent experience they are calling us to as a way to reach the unitive realm is revealed through a path of selfless service that is both purgative and illuminative.

Chapter Thirty-Six

Service as a Calling

One of the important concepts I learned from the spiritual literature of the East is the ancient tradition of enlightened helpers of humanity known as bodhisattvas.

These are the compassionate souls who, in every age, have attained the unitive experience to drink deeply of wisdom's cup. Then, not content to bask in Paradise while others suffer, they have hurried back to nurture those who are lost and thirsty, to share Spirit's golden elixir that does not dissipate when the soul has imbibed its sweetness.

A shining example of such an individual was George W. Russell (Æ) who understood that becoming the person he envisioned was dependent upon service to causes greater than himself.

Reviving the Ancestral Spirit

When I discovered the work of Æ, my Irish soul felt as if I had known him forever. His dedication to reviving Ireland's ancestral spirit of soul freedom appealed to my own love of Éire's history. I was moved by the mysterious, otherworldly aspects of his character, which many who knew him often glimpsed when he intoned the rhythmic cadences of his mystical poetry.

A remarkable fact about Æ is that, in true bodhisattva fashion, he surrendered the personal career he might have enjoyed as a gifted painter. Instead, he pursued active service to the Irish who desperately needed his inspiring visions of spiritual realms as well as his dedication to the independence of his homeland.

Episodes from his life repeatedly demonstrate that actions he took on behalf of others flowed from a soul calling. In biographies and articles about Russell, I have learned of countless events in which he would have preferred not to participate, except for his inner knowing that he was the best person for the job.

He was powerfully inspired to speak to and for Ireland, just as Maslow once said that he was compelled to overcome his own shyness in order to present his revolutionary theories. These wayshowers knew in their souls that they were born to make dramatic contributions to their age. And so, they spoke.

Transcending the Allure of Art
Before Russell assumed the pen name of Æ, he attended art school in Dublin, where his remarkable talent greatly impressed his fellow student William Butler Yeats.

Throughout Æ's life he continued to draw and paint as a way to replenish his energy and clarity of mind. And he did achieve some notoriety for his ethereal paintings that portrayed the numinous world that continually appeared to him.

However, in his early twenties he realized that being an artist was not going to support his development as a person. He assiduously studied sacred texts from East and West and eventually became a journalist and editor for two magazines, *The Irish Homestead* and later *The Irish Statesman*.

Along with his personal literary pursuits, he was a devoted champion of upcoming writers, many of whom became famous. He published their early works and gave them generously of his time, encouragement, and mentorship.

A gifted natural economist as well as an inspired poet, dramatist, and essayist, he became intensely involved in educating farmers in Ireland and America about how to form efficient cooperatives. He taught them to pool their resources and create economic independence through the rural banks he helped to establish.

Æ was also intimately connected with attempts to reconcile differences between political factions leading up to the treaty that split the country into Northern Ireland and the Irish Republic in the south. If leadership had followed his suggestions, the civil war "troubles" that ensued might have been largely avoided.

While he worked tirelessly for his country, Æ wrote poetry and prose inspired by his otherworldly visitations that continued unabated.

I have spent many inspiring hours immersed in Æ's mystical writings. His novel *The Avatars* is a deep dive into the "many-colored land" he experienced in the visions that bathed his soul. His autobiographical book, *The Candle of Vision*,[51] opens a window into how he transcended a youthful, egocentric preoccupation with his visions and learned to guide them into insights that uplifted many others.

Over the years he became convinced that only in service to humanity were such prodigious gifts as his truly useful. Despite his inability to turn egoic politicians into altruistic statesmen, his unwavering dedication to his country's freedom from tyranny earned him the love and respect of many who considered him the most important man in Ireland.

Æ's Message About Service

In an article titled "On the March," Æ has this to say about a lifetime spent in service. I can feel him speaking to anyone who may be questioning how to become a better person. He writes:

>...our being is inadequate if we do not blend heart with heart and flame with flame. Do not think because you are alone that you can accomplish nothing, for every thought and aspiration to the divine is something gained in the eternal struggle, a wandering fire captured and transmuted for the building in pure light of the temple of the eternal beauty.[52]

Following Æ's Example

I agree with Æ. While conducting personal development workshops or in spirited conversation with friends or strangers whom I have met in my travels, I have been graced with heart-to-heart connections like those he describes.

During these timeless intervals, my awareness has centered within a unity of presence where my attention is heightened in listening and responding, in asking and proposing.

In retrospect those conversations seemed to be taking place as a mystical exchange between my True Self and the other persons'. When the interaction was complete, everyone had been elevated. These were profoundly inspiring experiences that expanded my heart and revealed new opportunities for enhanced service.

After a recent book-signing event, I was literally swimming in so much love for other people that I felt as if I were seeing them with the eyes of the Divine.

I am convinced that Æ had many such experiences as he strove to uplift every person he encountered. In fact, I can sense him being aware that a compassionate spirit was gazing at his acquaintances through his own insightful perception of their souls.

Chapter Thirty-Seven

Transcending in the Unitive

George W. Russell (Æ) was a man of his time and his country. In fact, I cannot imagine his mission taking place anywhere other than in Ireland—for this home of the divine presence he called "The Mighty Mother" birthed and cradled his purpose.

The island's Gaelic name, Éire, is derived from the mythic goddess Ériu. The many wells one finds in Irish fields and shrines are reputed to be openings into the body of the goddess.

Every time I have visited the Emerald Isle,[53] I have felt the presence of the Mother in counties Clare and Kerry along the Wild Atlantic Way and in County Kildare in the Ancient East. Here an eternal flame burns where the bishop Brigid founded her dual monastery for women and men in the sixth century AD.

I have found the Irish culture rich with the presence of the Mother in soul-stirring music, myth, and a native gift for colorful speech. The Gaelic language sparks my imagination with metaphor and the contextual flavor of a people who, at least in the West, remain intimately connected to the soil that feeds my soul with every step I take across Éire's shimmering green landscape.

Communing with the Divine

Æ knew the Mighty Mother as the lover of the presence he called the Mystic Father. As bearer of the life the Mother brings forth, she is the fiery defender of their children. Æ himself was the grateful beneficiary of how she nurtures souls in all their seasons.

Mother of the World by Nicholas Roerich, 1930s

And he observed how, when their lifespan has expired, she is the one to bury the dead, welcoming their spent bodies back into her earthly womb so their souls may be reborn.

About the Mighty Mother, Æ wrote:

> She rewarded me by lifting for me a little the veil which hides her true face. To those high souls who know their kinship the veil is lifted, her face is revealed and her face is like a bride's.[54]

Understanding Æ

Æ cherished his communion with the Mother's creative spirit, which I sense helped him navigate living in the unitive experience of his visions while remaining grounded in the rigorous schedule he maintained for decades as economist and editor.

The lustrous images of his paintings and the word pictures he created in his poems and mystical writings reveal the inner man. His correspondence brims with the kindness and humor that endeared him to his many friends. The volumes of magazine articles he wrote demonstrate the acuity of mind that gave him unprecedented influence throughout Ireland and beyond.

And everything he created sent out sparks of illumination.

Spending many hours reading Æ's words, and what others have said about the accomplishments for which he honored the Mighty Mother, illustrates for me what it means to continue transcending in the unitive experience. The opportunities for growth and new learning are endless.

Like every enlightened wayshower before and after him, Æ's goal was to embody the True, the Good, and the Beautiful, to bring the light of mystical Being into the physical, and to awaken other souls to their personal, inherent brilliance.

Resolving the Opposites

I recently watched an interview with Irish writer James Tunney who has studied Æ extensively. He said that, as a mystic and student of ancient sacred texts, Æ anticipated Jung in recognizing the need for transmuting the subconscious and balancing the archetypal energies of the divine complements (Father/Mother) that together create universal oneness.

From his reading of Eastern literature and intuitive awareness of his own soul, Æ would have understood that our body is not our identity. Over the course of many lifetimes, our soul puts on masculine or feminine forms in order to master the sacred energies that exist in every part of life.

From my perspective as an entertainer, I see the process as a bit like performing in a musical revue. I will wear a variety of costumes while singing and dancing to many different tunes. Yet underneath, I remain the same performer. As a dramatist who was instrumental in founding the Abbey Theater in Dublin, Æ would have understood the similarity.

Especially in his poetry, I sense him reflecting upon the necessity of harmonizing the opposites that appear in the physical plane as key to attaining the wholeness that is the nature of the unitive. Because he was so aware of ethereal realms in which polarities do not exist, he tried to bring balance to any situation in which he found himself.

Accessing the Mother's Practicality

I have read that when our spiritual acuity is heightened, we have access to the practical know-how of the Divine Mother. This is the common-sense air that Æ breathed.

No matter who his listeners might be, he never failed to offer them inspired suggestions about how to improve their lot in life. The doing was their responsibility. Still, if they paid attention to how he was being, they would observe the shining star of a creative spirit in action—the Mother's know-how exemplified in the person of her son Æ.

Where others perceived only parts or manufactured dichotomies, Æ (like Maslow) saw unity and the potential for achieving it. His intention was always to elevate human discourse above the pettiness of polarities that he knew were fabrications of an unreal self.

One reason for his fame as a mediator was his ability to hear both sides of an argument and then clearly articulate back to those involved the essence of what each side wanted. Having gained their attention apart from their ideological bias, he was then able to offer a solution that could bring the parties together.

Confirmed adversaries, who in daily life might glare at each other across the abyss of Irish politics, found common ground at the weekend salons Æ held in his home. He welcomed anyone who was interested in his expositions upon the perennial philosophy's ancient wisdom, which he applied as equally to himself as to his fellow travelers on the path to the Eternal.

Following the Mother's Example

Æ understood his own soul's yearning to permanently transcend the limitations of time and space. And he personally experienced how the Mighty Mother extends her hand from the ethereal, many-colored land into physical dimensions, raising transcending souls to levels of higher consciousness.

Æ found himself following the Mother's example when, for several years, he brought his visions with him as he traveled into the poorest rural communities to teach desperate Irish farmers how to pull themselves out of poverty.

As his communion with the Mighty Mother deepened, he discovered his self-discipline and spiritual mastery increasing. He contacted a mystery that comes to mystics who achieve the unitive as a stage of personal development: Transcendence is the nature of mystical Being.

We May Likewise Enter In
Just as Æ perceived the Mother as a personal, dynamic, creative force that moved in, through, and around him, when we ourselves enter into the unitive, we are in a constant figure-eight flow between etheric and physical dimensions.

This is a characteristic that Maslow observed in his most psychologically mature subjects and is how our Wise Inner Counselor continues to illumine our soul. In its many guises, the spirit of transcendence is always in motion.

Messenger of the Ultimate Gift
Like Maslow, Wordsworth, Emerson, and thousands of mystics, Æ can be seen as a messenger for the essence of the True, the Good, and the Beautiful that he contained in his being.

This was the ultimate gift that he did his best to transmit to others. Many listened to him and some caught the vision of his gift. But many more did not.

Yes, they agreed that George Russell was the most important man in Ireland. They read his essays in *The Irish Homestead* and *The Irish Statesman*. They acknowledged his brilliance.

Yet in the end, the politicians and religious leaders who could have saved Ireland from the warring factions that tore her apart, closed their hearts to Æ's common-sense solutions and went their own way. Rather than choosing the path of harmony with the Mother's practicality that the selfless servant in their midst so ardently demonstrated in his own life, they opted for separation and the resulting political strife that lasted for decades.

Reading about this tragic era of Ireland's history, I grieved with Æ as he witnessed in the Irish civil war the same senseless, violent destruction and bloodshed that horrified Wordsworth about the French Revolution, and that Emerson lived through in the American Civil War.

These three earnest wayshowers each came to realize what Maslow would observe in the wars and conflicts of the early and mid-twentieth century:

> Until we learn to compassionately resolve the archetypal opposites within ourselves and then extend that love knowledge to others, the goal of *Eupsychia* (the good society) is not possible.

Running the Race for Our Souls

Since time immemorial mystical wayshowers have been misunderstood, misinterpreted, and prevented from accomplishing all they had planned to achieve before they sailed to Earth, "trailing clouds of glory."

Yet the life and legacy of Æ offers a clear example of how one person can make an enormous difference in this world by following the lead of his intuition and devotion to the wisdom of the Mighty Mother.

Today we have an opportunity to make our own unique contribution to life from our personal experience of the unitive that Æ and Maslow and many others have achieved.

We are living in an age of universal freedom. However, that freedom can be realized only when we develop new levels of self-mastery. We are being called to run the race for our souls' liberation as we have not run that race in the past.

For many of us, this is rather like taking remedial courses in subjects we did not pass as an undergrad while simultaneously pursuing a master's degree. Fortunately, the practical Mother has provided us with useful tools.

We can study our psyche through the lens of Maslow and the transpersonal psychologists who succeeded him. We can pour spiritual light into pockets of imbalance in multiple planes of our consciousness. We can follow the guidance of our Wise Inner Counselor to outpicture its unifying presence.

Maintaining the Thread of Contact

We have never needed these tools more than in this century. With an enormous influx of the Divine Mother's spiritual essence comes an increase in darkness that rises up to oppose her light with a virulence that threatens to overwhelm us.

The untransmuted subconscious of nations and individuals that has been hiding all of the disowned, dissociated aspects of a world's psyche is being driven to the surface by the accelerating presence of extraordinary light.

And, still, we know that old patterns can be transmuted and our souls liberated to become who we really are.

No matter what challenges we may face, Æ demonstrates that maintaining the thread of contact with the eternal verities he found in the perennial philosophy will carry us through difficult days and dark nights into the light of the numinous dimensions he inhabited in the presence of the Mighty Mother.

Chapter Thirty-Eight

Transcending with Your Soul's Twin

As we accelerate our self-transcendent awareness, our search for life's one great love may fade into the background. Or for some, the desire may grow in importance.

When we focus on reaching our ultimate union with the Eternal, we may eventually realize that the one truly great love is between our soul and the Divine. Yet, as many have intuited, our souls do have a twin whose essential identity mirrors our own, for we were created as two halves of the same whole.

I have written extensively about this relationship because I was blessed to experience it personally with my late husband, Stephen.[55] In that light I would like to share with you a meditation on the mystery of twin flames that is dear to my heart.

Radiant Life, Radiant Love

We dream of love. We sing of love. We thrill to the metaphor of love in ballroom dancing and pairs ice skating. We may not admit it, but in our heart of hearts, even the least romantic among us may long to be half of a divine partnership.

For we are made of love. From the Eros of our parents who conceived the body we wear and also from the pure beingness of Love whose offspring we have been since the beginning.

The Promise We Did Not Keep

Way back when (before we knew to count time), our souls were created in a single orb of light that divided into two identities containing the same essential soul blueprint.

We took our leave of unity and forged separate paths with the promise that we would always come back to each other—a promise we found difficult to keep. In fact, we probably have been apart more often than we have smiled across the dinner table at the face of our beloved other half.

Such is the journey of our souls. We are twins who share the same original blueprint, but who may have built very different identities from the same foundation. Even when we find each other, the going may be tough, as the struggle to discover who we are as a united pair challenges us to the core of who we are as individuals.

Giving All to Love

Perfect love does exist when we let it emerge from the inside, when we allow inner guidance to transform us into our most authentic Self, and when we choose to give all to Love so we may receive all in return.

This is the opportunity offered to each of us to ascend the mountain of wholeness on the trek we began long ago. When we surrender our egoic struggles, the summit can be attained. For that is where the ultimate reunion of twin flames is found and where perfect Love lasts forever.

How Twin Flames Can Connect

We are like snowflakes, utterly unique in all of creation. No two souls in cosmos contain the same pattern as ours.

Actualizing the highest aspects of our being means attracting those qualities into the physical through transmutation and embodying the virtues that are intrinsic to our True Self. The more we become equal to our soul essence, the more we become equal to the soul essence of our twin flame.

Of course, our soul's other half may not be in embodiment or available for a romantic relationship. And I can assure you that being married to your twin flame contains as many perplexities as being married to anybody else—possibly more—because the reuniting of twin souls is so mightily opposed.

We may not realize the potential power that can be released through our reunion on behalf of universal truth, goodness, and beauty. But malevolent forces are fully aware and seek to thwart our spiritual mastery at every turn.

So, we focus on being Love in action. We meditate on the presence of the divine spark within us and we let the light flow. All of the eternal verities we embody accrue to our twin flame, no matter where they are in time and space.

Although we may not meet in the physical, our souls will feel the connection.

A Journey of Twin Flames

In the beginning was the one—
a single spark that burst to flame,
then twinned to two as tongues of fire
sent forth in Love from Eternity's orb.

Made alike in spheres of light,
loved into being with one intent—
service always in their hearts,
these two agreed to sacrifice
the perpetual unity of their birth
to free up all of humanity.

Two bright halves of the same coin
always seeking Beauty and Truth
on behalf of the vibrant Good,
longing for reunion that can come
when angels finally clear the way.

For each must offer a balanced heart—
the original purpose which they forgot
yet will remember very soon,
in the many-colored land,
the home their souls know as their own.

Chapter Thirty-Nine

A Rhapsody of Transcendence

As I was completing these chapters whose purpose has been to strengthen the thread of contact with our innermost essence of Being, words like a rhapsody flew into my heart from my Wise Inner Counselor—the great lover of my soul and the source of a special wisdom that is joy.[56]

A Divine Romance
Throughout time enlightened mystic wayshowers have appeared with a passionate intention to reveal the soul's innate grandeur. For centuries they have portrayed transcending the lesser self as a divine romance between the soul and the Wise Inner Counselor that Æ called the "Magician of the Beautiful."

When we accept their perception, our daily life can be a dance of Love in action, as the inner guide woos the soul into its essence that is vibrant in the blood, warm in the heart, radiant in the mind, and beautiful beyond words.

The Ecstasy of Union
In that light we enter the unitive realm of active stillness where we are enfolded in such unspeakable sacredness that the soul's only prayer is praise.

Cradled in this numinous atmosphere we are untouchable, infinite, a child, an aged wise one. We feel our youth and our maturity. We are newborn and wizened elder.

Fresh as the dawn and ancient as the Earth whose pathways we have trod for eons, we move freely in cosmic consciousness with our will tethered to the Divine.

Here is the ecstasy of union that may occur to those who truly desire to be found in the timelessness of Being. Here our hearts burn in the sublime exultation of knowing ourselves as joyful travelers on a transcendent journey, living in ceaseless connection with who we really are.

An Invitation

"O fiery soul," declares the voice of Love. "Be a light unto the world until your mission is fulfilled, which completion may be closer than you think.

"You have become the sum that is greater than all your parts. You have shed all that was immature and fanciful. Now refined in the cleansing fires of the Great Alchemist, you are gold, indeed.

"Receive the boundless bounty of my presence," says the inner wise one, the Beloved. "Experience the allness of your Self. For we are one, and your luminous life is here."

Chapter Forty

Reflecting on Your Luminous Life - 5

And so, we have come to the end of our journey together where we must part ways, at least for now. These completions are always poignant. Still, we know they are also beginnings. A new pathway emerges, leading us to higher summits and deeper mysteries that are just waiting to be explored by fervent hearts.

In that light I would like to offer some final reflections on what the journey of self-transcendence has brought to my mind and heart during the writing of this book.

Storing Up Light
I have noticed that peak experiences may store up reservoirs of light in anticipation of our journey toward sublime summits.

As we have experienced, that trek may send us scrambling up rocky slopes or clearing dense undergrowth from the depths of our subconscious. We may battle fierce winds, turbulent seas, cloudy days, and dark nights.

Yet we continue with a courage not wholly our own because we have perceived a light that urges us onward.

We also have felt an incomparable joy, enfolded in a love so profound as to be ineffable, beyond knowing or speaking, except to say, "I am changed from what I was to what I am."

Imagining a Bright Future
If you are so inclined, a lovely way to help anchor your reflections

on how you might envision your luminous life unfolding in the future is to engage your creativeness.

You might want to assemble a vision board with sayings and images that inspire you. Draw or paint a picture. Write a story or a poem. Sing your favorite tunes or compose new ones.

Dance with the abandon of a child reveling in the freedom of movement. Create a video or audio or slide show of images that capture the felt sense of where you have been and where you are going.

I encourage you to let your soul's unique creativeness really shine here. I am confident that your reflections will be richer for the experience.

Part Six

Resources for Your Journey

More ~ For New Beginnings
Enhancing Your Transcendence
Being Transcendent & Resilient

Mountain Trail, Grand Teton National Park
Jackson, Wyoming

Chapter 41 - Appendix A

Enhancing Your Transcendence

Coming back to a felt sense of being grounded can be a challenge after engaging in deep reflection. Fellow travelers have often asked me for suggestions to help ease them into the next phase of their journey. This is a request I am happy to oblige with the following thoughts in the hope that they may be useful to you now and in the future of your luminous life.

1. Cherish Your Best Friend

I love my Wise Inner Counselor. I treasure our ongoing conversation as a precious gift. When I look back on my life, the events that really stand out are actually not those episodes of unmistakable warnings or strong directives that have instantaneously and dramatically changed the trajectory of my life.

Those connections are memorable. Yet what I cherish most are the subtle insights that appear as a sort of glimmer that points the way to exactly the next step I should take. A radiance exists in those moments that I perceive as a glow that is ever-so-brief and yet absolutely clear.

The miraculous nature of these encounters always amazes me and I am glad. I do not want to ever take them for granted because they are a grace. I strive to be worthy of each new beam of enlightenment and to be grateful that my Wise Inner Counselor and I are the best of friends.

2. Beautify Your Environment

The course I taught on critical thinking and creative problem solving made the point that creativity is environmentally sensitive. If you want to improve your ability to innovate, switch up your environment to correspond to your goals.

Do not expect to get fresh ideas in a cluttered office or dull conference room. Take team building to an inspiring location. Have fun. Play some games. Bring color, music, and art into the mix and watch how innovation begins to percolate.

Beauty awakens the soul and creates a forcefield of protection around the light you invoke into your surroundings, which enhances your transcendence.

Earlier this year I embarked upon a major home improvement project. I hired a talented handyman who ended up doing more repairs than I had any idea needed to be tackled. I planted flowers. Had the trees trimmed. Mowed my lawn more often. And eliminated clutter from every room in the house.

The result? I can feel my home and property vibrating with an energetic buoyancy I have never felt before.

3. Become an Alchemist of Spirit

How am I to comprehend the wholeness of the Divine when my ability to experience that wholeness is limited by the narrow lens of my perception?

If I can understand only the portion of inner wisdom that I can see, then to envision more, I must open the portals of my perception and let the light shine through.

And how do I accomplish so formidable a task?

"Empty your vessel of consciousness," says my Wise Inner Counselor. "Become an alchemist of Spirit and let the fires of transmutation burn away the dross of ego nonsense that prevents the light from penetrating your awareness."

I have learned that if I do not clear my mind and heart of obstructions, life has a way of doing it for me. And when I have allowed Spirit's transfiguring alchemy to change me, the losses I have experienced in life have become profound blessings.

Tests Will Come

Tests of our spiritual and psychological mettle are essential to the path of self-transcendence. This may be one reason why so few choose this way of being in the world. The rewards are many, yet they are often hard-won.

Not understanding cause and effect is a disadvantage. Unfortunately, many of our fellow travelers have not been told that adversities that seem to drop into life for no reason may have karmic origins. Having this knowledge allows us to take action to mitigate the negative circumstances we may encounter.

Actions We Can Take

We work on our psychology. We confront the shadow whenever it raises its crafty head. And we strive to continually improve.

We consider what people, places, and things we hold dear. Do they support our highest values and aspirations? Or are they attachments that keep us tethered to unhealthy worldviews?

These can be hard choices that we do not make casually. Still, I have learned many times over that anything I surrender that is real eventually comes back to me with greater mastery and richer blessing than I had thought possible.

A Story of Surrender

When I made the decision to join the spiritual community where I subsequently lived for nearly two decades, the thing I held most dear at the time was my career as a singer and actor. Although I had never been very successful, I still held out hope that a "big break" was just around the corner.

However, when Spirit called, I gave away my theatrical wardrobe, burned my publicity photos, resigned from a musical play in which I had just won the lead role, and drove straight to California to be with my teacher and her students.

For many years I was too busy to miss being on stage. Then one summer I and several other community members who had been professional entertainers were given the opportunity to start a performing group in a local dinner theater that catered to tourists visiting our area of southwestern Montana.

I discovered that I was a better actor and singer than ever. I was more centered in my heart, which seemed to give me access to greater skills than those I had given up. By the time we closed the dinner theater after several seasons, my desire to perform felt complete. Other projects took precedence and, in a way, I was relieved.

Since then I have always trusted that the Divine will refill my emptied vessel with its presence—which is the true gift.

4. Invoke Light into the Vacuum

When we empty ourselves by relinquishing elements of lesser consciousness through psychological or other means, we must immediately fill the void with light. Nature does abhor a vacuum.

I enjoy songs, chants, and mantras from a number of faith traditions. Still, the violet flame is my favorite agent for clearing the dross of ego substance and then replacing it with the spiritual energy that uplifts everything it touches.

This transmutative light sweeps my house clean when I use it. It is like a sacred wind that fills my sails with a vibration of love and wisdom, and it offers the great benefit of balancing karma. When I invoke this flame and others that complement its action of emptying and filling, I notice truly dramatic changes in my daily life.

5. Learn from Your Peak Experiences

One of the conundrums Maslow encountered in the early 1960s was that some people were intensely focused on the phenomena of peak experience, but not on psychological development.

These ecstatic episodes can trigger periods of profound introspection and deep psychological processing that require us to summon levels of spiritual mastery and determination that may seem impossible at the time. Not everyone wants to do that.

Maslow often emphasized that peak experiences are meant to be a catalyst to growth, not a conclusion in themselves. His psychologically mature transcenders treated these voyages into cosmic consciousness as stepping stones, not destinations.

Become the Mystery

Peak experiences can happen at any time to any one of any age. I see that mystery as an invitation to become a permanent resident of the Being-realm, rather than an occasional visitor.

Of course, I know that even in the unitive experience, the transcendent journey is never really complete. There are always higher and finer spheres of consciousness to reach. So, I do my best to never stop striving to internalize the light I invoke.

6. Stay the Course —Whether Long or Short

Being buoyed up by the spirit of transcendence is an exhilarating experience. In those moments we feel invincible. No challenge is too daunting as we rally to the cause of soul liberation for ourselves and others.

That is as it should be. Without our retaining the sense memory of ethereal contact, the hard work ahead might seem far beyond our capabilities. Still, we strive to complete the matter-in-hand, whatever it may be.

The journey of self-transcendence provides many reminders that graduation to the next level of Being does not occur until we have fulfilled the requirements of the level we are on. The challenge lies in knowing what constitutes fulfillment.

I have always been one who wants to skip ahead, and there have been times when it appeared that I did leap over others in line. The truth is that I had completed the step I was on. The time for change had arrived. And the requirements I had to meet at the new level stretched me in ways that often sent me to my knees in despair of ever being equal to the role that had appeared so easy in the glow of a new title.

Some assignments are brief and others may seem unendurably long. Regardless, we keep on keeping on until the prompting for a new direction lands in us with unmistakable clarity.

Attunement Is the Key

I recall the experience of a friend who was employed in a truly intolerable situation that she could not seem to leave, even though her health was beginning to be adversely affected.

She continued showing up for work until the supervisor who had been subtly mistreating her did something that was overtly vicious. In that single moment, my friend knew she was finished. She walked out of that office and never returned.

I was involved in a similar situation, although mine was not personally threatening. One day I simply ran out of work in a position I had expected to occupy for a couple of years.

I remember standing alone in my office and declaring, "I'm finished!" Within a week circumstances changed dramatically and I was propelled into an entirely new phase of my life that lasted for several years.

7. Practice Love Knowledge

I consider the practice of love knowledge to be one of the biggest take-aways from all of Maslow's vast body of work. The affectionate twinkle that distinguished him from those who tended to get stuck in their heads shines through his books and especially in his video interview with Warren Bennis from 1968.

With an IQ of 195, Maslow was often the smartest person in the room. But what really set him apart was his appreciation for the arts and culture and loving relationships that he said made life meaningful. He went into ecstasies over classical music and exuded a childlike delight in the presence of authenticity expressed by anyone.

I believe that is one reason for his emphasis on love knowledge. That essential quality of his Wise Inner Counselor simply radiated from him. When we cultivate a similar heartfelt regard for our fellow travelers, our work may likewise endure.

Chapter 42 - Appendix B

Being Transcendent & Resilient

We live in an age of unprecedented calamity. Some disasters are so-called "natural" events such as hurricanes, tornadoes, or the thousand-year flood of the Yellowstone River that swept through Montana in 2022. Other disasters are man-made through negligence or actual malfeasance.

Regardless of the source, these events have the potential to reduce families, businesses, and entire communities to rubble—throwing everyone involved into survival mode, the lowest level of Deficiency-needs on Maslow's hierarchy.

In these situations our priority is always the preservation of life and property. The thing to remember is that your momentum on previously fulfilled needs can aid you in regaining your equilibrium and finding the life force of resilience within your being.

The Ultimate Early-Warning System
Sometimes we simply must run for our lives, as in the case of devastating fires that have obliterated a number of communities in recent years. Deciding when, how, and where to evacuate can be a matter of attunement when agencies or authority figures have erected virtual or actual roadblocks to escape.

The fact that entire towns have been uninformed or misinformed about looming dangers is, to me, the number-one reason for each of us to develop a line of clear, intuitive communion with our Wise Inner Counselor.

Inner guidance is the ultimate early-warning system that can alert us before emergency sirens sound. Or when they don't. If we do not have this lifeline in place on a daily basis, we and our loved ones may face imminent peril. The equation in this age may be as basic as that.

More Than Bouncing Back

The capacity to rise above life's worst situations is vital to our survival. As self-transcenders we accept that we cannot return to a former way of living. We may rebuild after catastrophe, but life will never be the same.

And yet, the inexhaustible light of our Wise Inner Counselor continues to act as a fount of positive energy that can propel us forward in the face of the direst circumstance.

My own experience with loss taught me that tapping into my soul's native creativeness could initiate new waves of inspiration and open interior reservoirs of resilience that I never knew existed.

I also have found that inquiry engages that creativeness in very practical ways. My inner guide loves to answer questions.

Preparedness Through Inquiry

In my book *The LIGHT Process: Living on the Razor's Edge of Change*,[57] I proposed five questions that can be helpful to ask in times of major upheaval.

It may seen counter-intuitive to stop what you are doing and ask yourself questions when your world is going up in flames. Still, I have learned from experts in crisis management and disaster recovery that being able to step back from a situation that is fraught with anxiety may be the most effective way of moving through chaos.

To achieve a balanced response takes practice and prior awareness of your capabilities—which is another reason why I encourage developing an ongoing conversation with your Wise Inner Counselor who can detect the short-cuts, the escape routes, and the quickest way to safety in any situation.

I know this approach does not work for everyone. However, in the event that you might find this information useful, I am including my latest thinking about The LIGHT Process.

How Well Do You Know Yourself?

Are you conscious of the virtues, knowledge, competencies, and skills that you bring to any situation?

Although our physical world may have been decimated, we never really start from zero as far as our personal capabilities are concerned. One thing Maslow observed in his psychologically healthy subjects was how familiar they were with the talents they could easily activate in times of need.

After working for many years with an assessment model that identifies individual thinking style preferences,[58] I understand that we see the world as we are, not as it is. This is especially true in chaotic situations when emotions can swamp even the clearest thinkers.

We often see others much better than we see ourselves. If you are not sure of your top strengths, you might ask people who know you well. Finding out how others perceive where you add the greatest value can be very illumining.

It also can be helpful to know your weaknesses, although you may be very aware of those factors that have tripped you up in difficult situations. So, to remain focused on the positive, here are some descriptions to help you identify your talents:

- Are you a good analyzer of facts and situations, especially when precise thinking is essential?
- Do you notice details that others overlook, particularly of potential threats?
- Are you the one who immediately identifies and cares for the needs of others?
- Are you the big-picture, idea person who arrives at novel solutions?

Possessing this level of personal awareness can help you keep your head when others are losing theirs. This is where healthy self-esteem based on attunement with your Wise Inner Counselor can prevent you from falling into group-think. A frantic majority is not the best determiner of effective action.

What Do I Need Right Now?
This is the question I ask at least a dozen times a day when I am working on a writing project. I get so involved in trying to tune in to what belongs in the text that I sometimes lose track of time and the necessities of daily life.

To bring myself back to the physical plane, I ask my Wise Inner Counselor what's now, what's next, and what is the most important facet of the present moment that I should deal with.

Sometimes the priority is to do nothing except breathe, take a break, settle into my heart, and listen for the guidance that may have little to do with action. This is where the integration of being and doing is so important. And, again, the momentum we develop on that integration can be a life-saver.

I never leave my office (even to go for a walk) without a notepad and pen—or at least the ability to record a voice memo on my cell phone. My Wise Inner Counselor is very participative and loves to send me new ideas almost as soon as I change my physical location.

I also have found it useful to do a quick self-check for any subtle, unfulfilled Deficiency-needs that could detract from the presence of mind I want to maintain.

Sometimes those deficiencies only reveal themselves when I step away from the busyness of the day and give my inner child an opportunity to communicate her unmet needs.

How Strong Is My Thread of Contact?

I think the greatest danger to our self-transcendence is allowing a sense of separateness to creep into our consciousness. Making sure to strengthen the thread of contact with the divine spark in our heart can be a port in the storm.

This is another area where creating a momentum is key. Whatever you do to keep your equilibrium, you may want to engage in that practice regularly so you do not have to search for it when things go awry.

What Do I Need to Let Go Of?

Losing everything except the clothes on your back can be the most devastating experience any of us will face. Being stripped of all outer support can reduce us to primitive behaviors. Or it can provide the impetus for discovering inner resilience and the divine guidance that perhaps we had never contacted before.

In crisis situations we may need to let go of anxiety. This is one thing that inquiry and spiritual practice can help us do. At other times when change is not so dramatic, another way to phrase this question is: What is naturally letting go of me?

Much of effective self-transcendence involves allowing

change to happen. We do the inner work on our psychology and we invoke light into internal and external obstacles. Then we step back and allow Spirit to do its work.

Where Do I Go From Here?
Always to safety first. And then sometimes we find there is another portal just waiting for us to walk through to brighter tomorrows, even if today feels hopeless.

I am reminded of a scene from the film *Eat Pray Love* when Liz Gilbert (played by Julia Roberts) is praying to God for direction, perhaps for the first time in her life.

She is tearfully asking what she should do to resolve the chaos in her life. We wonder with her: What cosmic wisdom will be forthcoming in this desperate hour of her personal and professional crisis?

Yet the only thing she hears is, "Go back to bed, Liz."

Sometimes the most practical wisdom is the simplest. No fanfare. No roll of drums or dramatic voice-over. Just go back to bed. Or more likely, get out of bed and live today with all the vigor you can bring to it.

Making Progress Throughout Our Journey
Of course, we may not always hear a voice. In fact, as we ascend to greater heights of Being, we may not be as aware of hearing specific instruction as we are of simply acting in alignment with the inner guidance we have internalized.

To transcend the egoic self is to grow up, to choose as wisely as we are able, and then to take responsibility for those choices. This is the practical journey we pursue and the resilience we can achieve by being attuned to the unitive way of being in the world.

We may not completely escape terrible situations. Life on

planet Earth is fraught with unseen perils. And yet, I am convinced that we can find ultimate safety in the Eternal One that is our true Reality. This is why I am a lifelong learner pursuing the journey of self-transcendence.

I am comforted to know that the Divine does not deny us our successes. Instead, the presence of Universal Love celebrates with us. For the taste of victory is sweet—made sweeter still when shared and savored as both ending and beginning.

*Touching the transcendent,
we are lifted away
from our egoic self
into sublime unity
with the Spirit that we are.
Carry on!*

Notes

1. Learn more about the Wise Inner Counselor series at www.cheryleckl.com.

2. See Cheryl Lafferty Eckl, *A Beautiful Death: Keeping the Promise of Love* (Livingston, MT: Flying Crane Press, 2010, 2022, 2026) 4-5.

3. Abraham H. Maslow, *The Farther Reaches of Human Nature* (New York: Viking Press, 1971, published posthumously).

4. William Wordsworth, *Lines Written a Few Miles above Tintern Abbey, on Revisiting the Banks of the Wye during a Tour, July 13, 1798*.

5. Aldous Huxley, "Introduction" in *Bhagavad-Gita*, trans. Swami Prabhavananda and Christopher Isherwood (Hollywood: Vedanta Society of Southern California, 1944, 1951, 1987), xii-xiii.

   Summarizing the four basic tenets of the perennial philosophy:
   - The material plane of things and individual consciousness is a manifestation of a Divine Ground (the Absolute, Supreme Reality).
   - We have a dual nature: a temporal ego and an eternal self—the spark of divinity that lives in the spiritual heart.
   - Human beings can realize the existence of the Divine Ground by direct intuition through the agency of their inner divinity.
   - Our life on earth has only one purpose—to identify with the eternal Self and achieve union with the Divine Ground (the I AM).

6. Thomas Cahill, *How the Irish Saved Civilization: The Untold Story of Ireland's Heroic Role from the Fall of Rome to the Rise of Medieval Europe* (New York: Nan A. Talese/Doubleday, 1995).

7. See Eckl, *Reflections on Doing Your Great Work in Any Occupation* (Livingston, MT: Flying Crane Press, 2021, 2026).

8. Edward Hoffman, Ph.D, ed., *Future Visions: The Unpublished Papers of Abraham Maslow,* (Thousand Oaks: SAGE Publications, 1996), 178.

9. Henry Geiger (August 10, 1908 – February 15, 1989) was the editor, publisher, and chief writer of *MANAS Journal* which was published from 1948–1988.

10. Geiger, "Introduction: A. H. Maslow," in *The Farther Reaches of Human Nature*, xv.

11 Warren Gamaliel Bennis (March 8, 1925 – July 31, 2014) was an American scholar, organizational consultant and author, widely regarded as a pioneer of the contemporary field of leadership studies.

12 "Eulogy," by Warren Bennis in *Abraham H. Maslow: A Memorial Volume* (Belmont, CA: Wadsworth Publishing Company, 1972) 17.

13 Note from February 23, 1970 in *A Memorial Volume*, 100.

14 "In Memoriam of A. H. Maslow" by his colleague Professor Ricardo B. Morant in *Abraham H. Maslow: A Memorial Volume*, 27.

15 Geiger, in *The Farther Reaches*, xx.

16 Robert Frager, Ph.D. and James Fadiman, Ph.D., *Personality and Personal Growth*, 6th edition (Pearson Prentice Hall: 2005), 365-96.

17 Note from 1964, in *A Memorial Volume*, 63.

18 Ricardo B. Morant, "In Memoriam," 26.

19 Hoffman, *The Right to Be Human: A Biography of Abraham Maslow*, revised edition (New York: McGraw-Hill, 1999).

20 Maslow, *Motivation and Personality* (rev. ed.) (New York: Harper & Row, 1970), 150.

21 For a more complete list of general metapathologies, see *The Farther Reaches of Human Nature*, 307-09.

22 Maslow, "Cognition of Being in the Peak-Experiences" in *Toward a Psychology of Being* (Floyd, VA: Sublime Books, 2014), 66-68.

23 Ibid., 68.

24 Hoffman, *The Right to Be Human*, 122.

25 Maslow, *A Theory of Human Motivation*, 9.

26 See more about the Wise Inner Counselor and Esteem Needs in Eckl, *Reflections on Being Your True Self*, 107-19.

27 Maslow, *Toward a Psychology of Being*, 66.

28 Hoffman, *The Right to Be Human*, 314.

29 Maslow, *The Farther Reaches of Human Nature*, 14-18.

30 Geiger, in *The Farther Reaches*, xv.

31 See Howard Gardner, *Truth, Beauty, and Goodness Reframed: Educating for the Virtues in the Twenty-First Century* (New York: Basic Books, 2011). A prescient book by an eminent educator that deserves careful reading in light of the value-challenged intellectual climate that developed later in the first quarter of the twenty-first century.

32 See Wisdom as a core value in *Reflections on Being Your True Self,* 39-46.

33 Frager and Fadiman, 393.

34 Geiger, in *The Farther Reaches,* xx.

35 Maslow, *Religions, Values, and Peak-Experiences* (New York: Penguin Books, 1970), 13.

36 For a thorough exploration of reincarnation, see *Reincarnation: The Phoenix Fire Mystery—An East-West Dialogue on Death and Rebirth from the Worlds of Religion, Science, Psychology, Philosophy, Art, and Literature, and from Great Thinkers of the Past and Present,* compiled and edited by Joseph Head and Sylvia Cranston (Pasadena: Theosophical University Press, 1977, 1994)

37 Ruth Small, Ph.D., "The Roots of Vedanta in America" <https://american-vedantist.org/2018/articles/the-roots-of-vedanta-in-america/>(Accessed 4-20-2026)

38 Wordsworth, *Ode: Intimations of Immorality from Recollections of Early Childhood,* published 1807.

39 Emerson, *Compensation,* Essay III in *Essays: First Series.*

40 See https://www.violetflame.com/

41 See "A Glimmering Sense of Purpose" in Eckl, *Poetics of Soul & Fire* (Livingston, MT: Flying Crane Press, 2015), 111.

42 Eckl, *Reflections on Being Your True Self,* 76-82.

43 The perfect double helix was reportedly completed in 1878 by a mysterious carpenter who built the stairs without nails or external support and then disappeared. Modern engineers remain baffled by how the staircase was made. <https://www.lorettochapel.com/staircase> (Accessed 4-20-2026)

44 See https://www.cheryleckl.com/

45 Æ, *The Candle of Vision* in *The Descent of the Gods: The Mystical Writings of G. W. Russell - A.E.*, Raghavan Iyer & Nandini Iyer, eds. (Buckinghamshire, England: Colin Smythe Ltd, 1988), 89.

46 *New Era Community 1926* (New York: Agni Yoga Society, Inc., 1951), 182.

47 See "An Experience in Cosmic Consciousness" in Paramahansa Yogananda, *Autobiography of a Yogi* (Los Angeles: Self-Realization Fellowship, 1981, 1998, 2007) 165-173.

48 Emerson, *The Over-Soul*, Essay IX in *Essays: First Series*, published 1841.

49 Quoted in Henry Summerfield, *That Myriad Minded Man: A Biography of G. W. Russell: A.E.* (Buckinghamshire, England: White Crow Books in association with Colin Smythe, Ltd., 1975, 2023), 26.

50 Saint John of the Cross, *The Spiritual Canticle*, in *The Collected Works of St. John of the Cross*, trans. Kieran Kavanaugh and Otilio Rodriguez (Washington, DC: ICS Publications, 1979), 415.

51 *The Avatars* and *The Candle of Vision* are included in *The Descent of the Gods*.

52 Ibid, 644. For an example of what Æ means, see his short story titled "The Meditation of Ananda," in *Descent of the Gods*, 210-13.

53 See Eckl, *Sparks of Celtic Mystery: soul poems from Éire* (Livingston, MT: Flying Crane Press, 2019).

54 Æ, *The Candle of Vision*, 96.

55 Eckl, *A Beautiful Death* (2012) and *Reflections on Ineffable Love: from loss through grief to joy* (Livingston, MT: Flying Crane Press, 2022, 2026).

56 "Joy is a special wisdom." This beautiful phrase from the heart of a beloved master speaks deeply to my soul. See *New Era Community 1926*, 136.

57 Eckl, *The LIGHT Process: Living on the Razor's Edge of Change* (Livingston, MT: Flying Crane Press, 2013.)

58 The Herrmann Brain Dominance Instrument (HBDI). See https://www.thinkherrmann.com/ (Accessed 4-20-2026)

Stephen and me

Acknowledgements

To every person I have known, to fellow travelers whose conversation I have enjoyed, to students in my courses and workshops, to faces in the crowd of humanity, to my faithful colleagues Theresa and Michael McNicholas, James Bennett, and Paula Kehoe, and to you, dear reader—thank you for our encounters.

In great ways and small, all are enduring. I am who I am today because we have passed this way together.

Truly, we are citizens in an age of opportunity where we may live, learn, love, and give the gifts our souls long to share. And, ultimately, where we may create our own *Eupsychia*—the healthy society that fosters soul growth, love knowledge, mercy, and forgiveness.

My heart sings in deepest gratitude for my late husband, Stephen, for the generous wisdom masters who champion our path, and for my Wise Inner Counselor—the divine presence in my heart who gives me courage, strength, faith, and hope that I may live a luminous life in this world and the next.

I am beholden to the tireless saints, sages, seers, mystics, and solitary sojourners who have never stopped blazing the trail of self-transcendence, one illumined person at a time. They have left us maps so we might find ourselves united forever in the heart of the ever-expanding, universal, Eternal One.

For the possibility of this vision coming true, I am grateful.

About the Author

Since early childhood Cheryl Lafferty Eckl has exuded a zest for life. As a singer and actress she used her dramatic and comedic skills to delight musical theater audiences across the United States.

When she turned her attention to helping others as a professional development trainer, a new audience was equally receptive—this time to her unique insights into life's inevitable changes.

An engaging and knowledgeable speaker and teacher, for several decades she has delivered her practical wisdom with intelligence, humor, and real-life stories that shine a light on how you can become who you really are.

Cheryl is a lifelong student of the mystical traditions of East and West. She holds a master's certificate in Transpersonal Psychology and continues to write from her home in Livingston, Montana, where big skies and lofty mountains inspire her life and work with her own Wise Inner Counselor.

Learn more about her books, videos, and audios
at www.CherylEckl.com

www.ingramcontent.com/pod-product-compliance
Lightning Source LLC
Chambersburg PA
CBHW071232080526
44587CB00013BA/1577